A STORY IS Told

Inspiring Stories and
Illustrations from
OUR DAILY BREAD

Compiled by
DAVE BRANON

DISCOVERY HOUSE
PUBLISHERS®

Feeding the Soul with the Word of God

A Story Is Told
©2010 by RBC Ministries
All rights reserved.

Discovery House Publishers is affiliated with RBC Ministries,
Grand Rapids, Michigan.

Requests for permission to quote from this book should be directed to:
Permissions Department, Discovery House Publishers,
P.O. Box 3566, Grand Rapids, MI 49501, or contact us by e-mail at
permissionsdept@dhp.org

Interior design by Sherri L. Hoffman

Library of Congress Cataloging-in-Publication Data

A story is told : inspiring stories and illustrations from Our
daily bread / compiled by Dave Branon.
    p.   cm.
    1. Christian life—Miscellanea. I. Branon, Dave. II. Our
daily bread.
    BV4515.3.S86 2010
    242'.5—dc22   2010040457

Printed in the United States of America
Second printing in 2012

CONTENTS

Introduction 4

Aging 7

Anger 9

Bible 11

Christian Life 16

Christmas 23

Church and Worship 25

Comfort in Trials 29

Courage 31

Creation 34

Culture 38

Death 40

Facts and Trivia 44

Faith 47

Family 50

Fear 55

Forgiveness 57

Friendship 59

Giving 61

God 65

God's Guidance 67

God's Love 71

God's Presence 73

Grace 75

Heaven 77

Helping Others 79

History 83

Humor 85

Integrity 90

Jesus 92

Life 98

Love 99

Money 101

Neighbors 103

Perseverance 105

Prayer 107

Pride 112

Reconciliation 113

Resolutions 114

Resurrection 115

Sacrifice 118

Salvation 119

Sanctification 126

Satan 128

Service 130

Sin and Confession 133

Spiritual Gifts 139

Temptation 141

Testimony 143

Thankfulness 148

Trusting God 150

Warning 151

Wisdom 154

Our Daily Bread Writers . . .159

INTRODUCTION

"Where do you get your stories?" That is one of the questions asked most frequently of *Our Daily Bread* writers. And the answer depends on the writer. Each *ODB* writer dips into a different well for his or her "stories" that illustrate biblical truth. One writer seeks out stories from science or the world of exploration. Another examines popular culture to find current songs, sports anecdotes, or other examples that can be used to point toward truth. Still another tells stories that relate to family. It's a mixed bag of sources that, when combined, gives *Our Daily Bread* a breadth of experience that can touch people from all walks of life, from all cultures, from all backgrounds.

Each writer examines life and life events through a lens of biblical knowledge and through years of knowing God and living for Him. That way he or she can combine godly truth with mundane experience to craft an article that appeals to many people. It's the beauty of the *Our Daily Bread* devotional; it takes the reality of life and ties it into the reality of the divine.

When Henry Bosch and Dr. M. R. De Haan first crafted the initial *Our Daily Bread* articles back in the mid 1950s, they slowly discovered this formula of tying together life analogies and scriptural teaching. The first *Our Daily Bread* story appeared in the tenth article in the booklet, on April 10, 1956, written by Bosch, the first editor of the booklet:

> A famous traveler tells the story of how he and his party once tried to climb one of the highest peaks of the Sierra Nevada Mountains. "After infinite difficulty, exertion, and peril," he says, "we finally succeeded in surmounting the last precipice, and reached the summit, only to find on the opposite side the tracks of a wagon and the traces of a social feast!" If only he had taken the other side of the mountain he would have found an easily traveled

road all the way up! How like this foolish explorer are many Christians.

On July 1, 1956, Dr. De Haan told this poignant story, which was repeated many times in later articles:

> Some years ago I read an account which so touched my heart that I have never forgotten it. I do not remember where I read it, or who the author was, but it went something like this. A party of scientists and botanists were exploring certain otherwise inaccessible regions of the Alps in search of new species of flowers. One day they spied through a field glass a flower of such rarity and beauty that its value to science was incalculable. But it lay deep in a ravine with perpendicular cliffs on both sides. To get the flower someone must consent to be lowered over the cliff, a danger which was tremendous. A native lad who was curiously watching nearby and wondering what the scientists were doing was approached, and they suggested to him, "We will give you Five Pounds if you will let us lower you to the valley below and get that flower, and then we will pull you back up again." The little lad took one long look down the steep, dizzy depths, and then said, "Just a moment, and I'll be back," and ran away. A little later he returned followed by a gray-headed, stoop-shouldered old man, and approaching the botanist, the boy said, "I'll go over that cliff and get that flower for you if this man holds the rope. He's my dad."

That could be the prototypical *ODB* story. It has heart. It has drama. And it reveals an important truth by analogy: We can do life's hard parts if we know that God is "holding the rope."

Over the years, stories in the tradition of Dr. De Haan's vintage illustration became the heart of the *ODB* article. These stories can help us understand, process, and apply Bible truth to our lives in a way that makes each new article an adventure.

In this book, we honor the wisdom of the founders of *ODB* and the loyalty of *ODB* readers by providing in one volume three hundred stories that can guide us to know God better, to understand His Word more completely, and to enjoy the variety of wonder in the world He has given us. Arranged by topic, these stories can be used in a variety of ways. Pastors can use them for illustrations. Parents can use them for teachable moments. Sunday school leaders can use them as starting points for discussion. Educators can use them as elements of writing exercises. And all of us can use them as reminders of the relevance of God's truth and wisdom.

Some of the stories are humorous. Some are poignant. Some are informational. And all can be both interesting and edifying.

Read them. Learn from them. Share them. And perhaps someday, someone will say to you, "Where do you get your stories?"

AGING

GROW OLD WITH ME! THE BEST IS YET TO BE.
—ROBERT BROWNING

"Perls" of Wisdom

Those who wait on the Lord shall renew their strength. —*Isaiah 40:31*

Americans spend more than $20 billion annually on various anti-aging products that claim to cure baldness, remove wrinkles, build muscle, and renew the powers of youth. Can those products deliver what they promise? Dr. Thomas Perls of Boston University School of Medicine says there is "absolutely no scientific proof that any commercially available product will stop or reverse aging." (DM)

Too Old?

You are the light of the world.   —*Matthew 5:14*

God has limitless ways of reaching people. So if you feel that you don't have the ability to reach others for Christ, think about seventy-six-year-old Ethel Hatfield. Desiring to serve her Lord, she asked her pastor if she could teach a Sunday school class. He informed her that he thought she was too old! She went home heavy-hearted and disappointed.

Then one day as Ethel was tending her rose garden, a Chinese student from the nearby university stopped to comment on the beauty of her flowers. She invited him in for a cup of tea. As they talked together, she had the opportunity to tell him about Jesus and His love. He returned the next day with another student, and that was the beginning of Ethel's ministry. (VG)

What's Your Focus?

The things which are seen are temporary, but the things which are not seen are eternal. — *2 Corinthians 4:18*

A company boasted that its anti-aging cream could "banish" wrinkles and was asked to prove it in court. Findings showed that the cream did tighten skin, but only temporarily. The wrinkles were soon obvious again. Millions of people swallow such wild claims because they've believed the myths behind them: that the aging process is unacceptable and that undoing it is possible. The focus is on visible effects—all temporary—which is discouraging for those who trust in them.

In 2 Corinthians 4:16, Paul emphasized that physical decline is inevitable. He said, "Our outward man is perishing." But Paul didn't lose heart. Here's why: "The inward man is being renewed day by day." (JY)

The Aging Process

Do not cast me off in the time of old age; do not forsake me when my strength fails. —*Psalm 71:9*

ODB writer Bill Crowder was having breakfast with a friend who had recently celebrated his sixtieth birthday. They discussed the "trauma" of the number 6 being the first digit in his age and all that the age of sixty implies (retirement, Social Security, etc.). They also pondered the fact that he felt so much younger than such a "large" number would seem to indicate.

Then the conversation turned to the lessons, joys, and blessings he'd found in living those sixty years, and he said, "You know, it isn't really that bad. In fact, it's pretty exciting." The lessons of the past had brought a change in how he viewed the present. (BC)

ANGER

PEOPLE WHO FLY INTO A RAGE ALWAYS MAKE
A BAD LANDING. —WILL ROGERS

No Grudges after Sundown

Do not let the sun go down on your wrath. —*Ephesians 4:26*

A little boy got into a fight with his brother, and the whole experience left him feeling bitter. When his brother wanted to make things right, he refused to listen. In fact, he would not speak to his brother all day.

Bedtime came, and their mother said to the boy, "Don't you think you should forgive your brother before you go to sleep? Remember, the Bible says, 'Do not let the sun go down on your wrath'" (Ephesians 4:26). The boy looked perplexed. He thought for a few moments and then blurted out, "But how can I keep the sun from going down?"

The boy reminds us of some Christians. They're angry with certain people and hold grudges. When they are confronted with their unforgiving attitude and urged to make things right, they sidestep the issue and refuse to heed the clear instruction of Scripture. (RD)

History of a Murder

The beginning of strife is like releasing water; therefore stop contention before a quarrel starts. —*Proverbs 17:14*

The newspaper reported a tragic incident of violence that took place in a South American country. A peasant killed his best friend while they were arguing about political differences. When asked why he did it, he replied with these chilling words: "We began peacefully, and then we argued. I killed him when I ran out of words."

This tragedy calls to mind Jesus' teaching in Matthew 5 about the close connection between anger and murder. (MD)

Peacemakers

Blessed are the peacemakers, for they shall be called sons of God.
—*Matthew 5:9*

Eric Liddell, the Scottish runner whose life was portrayed in the movie *Chariots of Fire,* served as a missionary in China for twenty years—the last two in a Japanese internment camp during World War II. He was known as a peacemaker among individuals and groups whenever anger flared in the stressful environment of the camp. Liddell's life left a deep impression on everyone.

When a Japanese guard asked why Liddell was not at roll call one day, a man told him that Eric had died unexpectedly a few hours earlier. The guard paused, then replied, "Liddell was a Christian, wasn't he?"

Liddell spoke no Japanese; the guard spoke no English. Their only direct contact was at the required roll calls, twice a day. How did the guard know that Liddell was a Christian? He must have seen Christ in Eric as he resolved conflicts in the camp. (DM)

Danger: Explosives

The discretion of a man makes him slow to anger, and his glory is to overlook a transgression. —*Proverbs 19:11*

A man from Michigan was helping remove a tree stump from his friend's yard. He decided to use some dynamite he had stored away in his house. It did the trick. The stump came out. But the explosion turned the stump into an airborne missile that traveled 163 feet before crashing through a neighbor's roof. The stump opened a three-foot hole in the neighbor's roof, split the rafters, and pushed through the ceiling of the dining room.

If we are honest, sometimes something similar happens in our lives. We use explosive words and actions to try to solve problems, but these only make things worse. We get action, but we leave a lot of damage in our wake. (MD)

——————————— Going Straight ———————————

First be reconciled to your brother, and then come and offer your gift. —Matthew 5:24

How far would you travel to put things right with a brother who hadn't spoken to you in ten years? Would you go three hundred miles from Iowa to Wisconsin? On a riding lawn mower?

Unable to drive a car and despising bus travel, Alvin Straight did exactly that in the intriguing film *The Straight Story*. It is the true-life drama of a seventy-three-year-old man who decided it was time to end the silence, stop the hating, and break down the wall of anger he and his brother had built between them.

Is there a relative, a friend, or a brother or sister in Christ with whom you need to make things right? Then why not go straight to that person and do it today? (DM)

BIBLE

I BELIEVE THE BIBLE IS THE BEST GIFT GOD HAS EVER GIVEN TO MAN. ALL THE GOOD FROM THE SAVIOR OF THE WORLD IS COMMUNICATED TO US THROUGH THIS BOOK.
—ABRAHAM LINCOLN

——————————— Rosetta Stone ———————————

The mystery of Christ, which in other ages was not made known to the sons of men ... has now been revealed by the Spirit. —Ephesians 3:4–5

For centuries, the hieroglyphic word pictures painted on Egyptian ruins were a mystery. Then in 1799 a French archaeological expedition at the Egyptian harbor of Rosetta discovered an ancient stone. It weighed 1,676 pounds and reflected beautiful dark gray, blue, and pink hues. But that is not what made it valuable.

The stone was inscribed with an identical message in different ancient scripts. Among them were hieroglyphics and classical Greek. Using Greek to translate, scholars soon understood the meaning of the hieroglyphics. They were no longer a mystery.

The Bible also contains an ancient mystery. For centuries it seemed that God's purposes were limited to the Jews. Yet with the appearance of Jesus of Nazareth, the meaning behind God's promise to Abraham to bless the whole world was revealed (Genesis 12:1–3). (DF)

The Lost Book

And Hilkiah the high priest said to Shaphan the scribe, "I have found the Book of the Law in the house of the Lord." —2 Kings 22:8

Two U.S. Senate staffers were cleaning out a storeroom underneath the Capitol when they spotted a partially opened door nearby. Curious, they stepped inside and found a small room jammed with dusty old brochures and payroll records. A leather-bound book with gold lettering caught their attention: Senators' Compensation and Mileage. It bore the dates 1790–1881.

What a find! It was a one-of-a-kind record of every dollar paid to senators during the Senate's first ninety years. Plus, the book contains the handwritten signatures of founding fathers Thomas Jefferson and John Adams. "The book speaks volumes," says historian Richard Baker. "There is nothing that comes remotely close to it in the archives of the Senate."

We can imagine that Hilkiah the high priest felt even more excitement when he discovered the long-lost "Book of the Law" in some hidden cranny in the temple. (DE)

Erasmus

Your word was to me the joy and rejoicing of my heart. —Jeremiah 15:16

For centuries, many Christians were not permitted to read God's Word in their own language. Instead, they were encouraged to attend Latin church services that few could understand.

Then, in 1516, the Dutch scholar Erasmus compiled and published the first New Testament in the original Greek language. This landmark work was the basis for the later publication of Luther's German Bible, Tyndale's English Bible, and the King James Version. These translations made the Scriptures understandable to millions of people around the world.

Erasmus could not have known the influence his Greek New Testament would have, but he did have a passion for getting its message to laypeople from all walks of life. In the preface he wrote: "I would have [the Gospels and the Epistles] translated into all languages... I long for the plowboy to sing them to himself as he follows the plow [and] the weaver to hum them to the tune of his shuttle." (DF)

Shakespeare's Translation

No prophecy of Scripture is of any private interpretation. —2 Peter 1:20

Some have speculated that William Shakespeare helped translate the King James Bible. They say that he inserted a cryptogram (a message written in code) while he translated Psalm 46. In this psalm, the forty-sixth word from the beginning is *shake* and the forty-sixth word from the end is *spear*. Furthermore, in 1610, while the King James Bible was being translated, Shakespeare would have been forty-six years old. Despite these coincidences, no serious evidence supports this theory.

Some people also claim to have found hidden meanings when interpreting the Bible. Certain cults will cite a verse out of context, which can then lead others into heretical doctrine. Some quote John 14:16, for example, and say that the "Helper" refers to their "new revelation." When compared with other

Scripture, however, the Helper whom Jesus sent to us is obviously the Holy Spirit (John 16:7–14; Acts 2:1–4).

The apostle Peter wrote, "No prophecy of Scripture is of any private interpretation." (DF).

The Truth about Truth

Always learning and never able to come to the knowledge of the truth. —2 Timothy 3:7

In 1692, Harvard College adopted as its motto *Veritas Christo et Ecclesiae*—"Truth for Christ and the Church." Its crest showed three books, with one face down to symbolize the limitation of human knowledge. But in recent decades that book has been turned face up to represent the unlimited capacity of the human mind. And the motto has been changed to *Veritas*—"Truth."

The pursuit of knowledge is praiseworthy, yet learning can quickly lead to pride and a refusal to acknowledge any limits on our mental abilities. When that happens, biblical truth is ignored or rejected. (VG)

The Law in the Heart

[They] show the work of the law written in their hearts. —Romans 2:15

Marilyn Laszlo dedicated her life to giving the Hauna people of New Guinea the Bible in their own language. As she worked on the translation, she came to the word for "sin." When Marilyn asked the people what they thought sin was, they told her, "It's when you lie." "It's when you steal." "It's when you kill." "It's when you take another man's wife."

Marilyn was astounded. They were giving her God's standards as spelled out in the Ten Commandments. "God's law is written on the heart of man," she later commented, underscoring the truth found in Romans 2:14–15.

What a remarkable verification of biblical truth! (DB)

Mom's Translation

Ezra had prepared his heart to seek the Law of the Lord, and to do it, and to teach statutes and ordinances in Israel. —Ezra 7:10

Four pastors were discussing the merits of the various translations of the Bible. One liked a particular version best because of its simple, beautiful English. Another preferred a more scholarly edition because it was closer to the original Hebrew and Greek. Still another liked a contemporary version because of its up-to-date vocabulary.

The fourth minister was silent for a moment, then said, "I like my mother's translation best." Surprised, the other three men said they didn't know his mother had translated the Bible. "Yes," he replied. "She translated it into life, and it was the most convincing translation I ever saw." (AC)

The Forgotten Book

I will never forget Your precepts, for by them You have given me life. —Psalm 119:93

A young boy noticed a large black book covered with dust lying on a high shelf. His curiosity was aroused, so he asked his mother about it. Embarrassed, she hastily explained, "That's a Bible. It's God's book." The boy thought for a moment and then said, "Well, if that's God's book, why don't we give it back to Him? Nobody around here uses it anyway." (RD)

Word Hunger

As newborn babes, desire the pure milk of the word, that you may grow thereby. —1 Peter 2:2

ODB writer Bill Crowder had just completed a night of Bible conference ministry in Kuala Lumpur, Malaysia, and was chatting with some of the people who had attended. At the end of the line was a young man in his twenties. He shared with Bill that he had been a Christ-follower for only about four months, and he was eager to learn more of the teachings of the Bible. Bill referred him to the RBC Web site with the Discovery Series topics as one possible resource for his personal study.

The next night the young man returned to the conference and shared that he had stayed up until 3:30 a.m. reading and processing the biblical truths he discovered in that online resource. With a big smile on his face, he declared that he just couldn't get enough of God's Word (1 Peter 2:2).

What spiritual hunger! (BC)

CHRISTIAN LIFE

WE MUST NEVER FORGET THAT TRUE CHRISTIANITY IS MORE THAN TEACHING—IT IS A WAY OF LIFE. —RAY STEDMAN

A Hill Too High

Do not worry about tomorrow, for tomorrow will worry about its own things. —Matthew 6:34

ODB writer Dave Branon and his wife Sue like to rollerblade. Near the end of one of their favorite routes is a long hill. When they first started taking this route, Dave tried to encourage Sue by saying, "Are you ready for the hill?" just before pushing their way to the top. But one day she said, "Could you please not say that? You make it sound like a huge mountain, and that discourages me."

It was better for Sue to face the hill thinking only about one step, or one rollerblade push, at a time instead of an entire steep hill to conquer.

Life can be like that. If we peer too far ahead of today, the challenges may feel like a Mount Everest climb. They can appear impossible to handle if we think we have to be "ready for the hill." (DB)

Rust Bucket

But you, O man of God, flee these things and pursue righteousness, godliness, faith, love, patience, gentleness. —*1 Timothy 6:11*

On June 15, 1957, a brand-new car was buried in a concrete vault under the courthouse lawn in Tulsa. In June 2007, the car was unearthed as the city celebrated Oklahoma's 100th year of statehood. Writing in the *Tulsa World*, Randy Krehbiel said: "Now we know what 50 years in a hole does to a Plymouth Belvedere." Water seeping into the vault had turned the once shiny car into a rusted monument to the past. A hot-rod expert hired to start the engine pronounced it "hopeless."

Spiritual inactivity corrodes the soul like moisture acting on metal. (DM)

Check the Obvious

Even as Christ forgave you, so you also must do. —*Colossians 3:13*

When Bill Husted walked into his fortieth high school reunion, he shook hands and hugged people for twenty minutes before realizing there were two high school reunions in the building that day, and he was at the wrong one.

Husted, a technology writer for the *Atlanta Journal-Constitution*, used that experience to illustrate one of his enduring axioms of computer troubleshooting: Check the obvious first. Before you replace the sound card, make sure the volume control is not turned down. If the modem isn't working, check to see if it's connected.

"Check the obvious first" can be a good principle for spiritual troubleshooting as well. (DM)

Hearing and Doing

Be doers of the word, and not hearers only, deceiving yourselves.
—James 1:22

A man in New York City died at the age of sixty-three without ever having had a job. He spent his entire adult life in college. He had acquired so many academic degrees that they looked like the alphabet behind his name.

Why did this man spend his entire life in college? When he was a child, a wealthy relative died who had named him as a beneficiary in his will. It stated that he was to be given enough money to support him every year as long as he stayed in school. And it was to be discontinued when he had completed his education.

The man met the terms of the will, but by staying in school indefinitely he turned a technicality into a steady income for life—something his benefactor never intended. Unfortunately, he spent thousands of hours listening to professors and reading books but never "doing." (RD)

The Frog's Blackboard

Turn away my eyes from looking at worthless things, and revive me in Your way. *—Psalm 119:37*

As a young boy, one of Mart De Haan's favorite pastimes was hunting frogs along the banks of a pond near his home. But he was unaware of their unique visual powers that enabled them to elude him so easily. Later he learned that the frog's optical field is like a blackboard wiped clean, and that the only images it receives are objects that directly concern it. These little amphibians are never distracted by unimportant things, but are aware only of essentials and whatever may be dangerous to them.

What a good reminder for us not to be distracted by unimportant things—not to become preoccupied with the vain things of the world. (MD)

Limited but Useful

I was with you in weakness, in fear, and in much trembling.
—*1 Corinthians 2:3*

Suzanne Bloch, an immigrant from Germany, often played chamber music with Albert Einstein and other prominent scientists. She said that Einstein, though an accomplished violinist, irritated his fellow musicians by not coming in on the beat. "You see," Bloch explained, "he couldn't count." Einstein could project revolutionary theories about the cosmos, but he had difficulty with rhythmic counting. Despite his limitation, he remained an enthusiastic musician.

Do we sometimes lament our limitations? We all have abilities, but we are also afflicted with inabilities. We may be tempted to use our limitations as an excuse for not doing the things God has enabled us to do. Just because we may not be gifted to speak in public or to sing in a choir doesn't mean that we can sit on the spiritual sidelines doing nothing. (VG)

Rocks and Robots

When I consider Your heavens, the work of Your fingers, the moon and the stars... what is man that You are mindful of him? —*Psalm 8:3–4*

During a walk through the picturesque Garden of the Gods in Colorado Springs, *ODB* writer David McCasland's attention was diverted from the huge, majestic, sandstone rocks toward two people wearing homemade robot suits. The park was thronged with summer tourists who immediately began taking pictures of the robots while their children gathered round to touch and talk to them. Folks who had come to admire the silent beauty of God's creation were now watching people in cardboard costumes sprayed with silver paint.

David said the sight reminded him of his quiet time. "How often I sit down to seek the Lord through Bible reading and prayer, only to be drawn away by the newspaper, an unpaid bill, or a list of things to be done." (DM)

Are You a Complainer?

When the people complained, it displeased the Lord. —Numbers 11:1

A farmer was known for his negative attitude. One day a neighbor stopped by and commented on the farmer's wonderful crop. "You must be extremely happy with this year's harvest," he said. The farmer grudgingly replied, "Well, yes, it looks like a pretty good one, but a bumper crop is awfully hard on the soil." (RD)

Visible Reminders

These words which I command you today shall be in your heart.
—Deuteronomy 6:6

A growing number of people find that wearing a pedometer helps them increase their level of daily exercise. The step-counting device is both a recorder and a motivator for them. Knowing how many steps they take encourages them to walk more.

One woman, whose goal was to take ten thousand steps a day, began parking farther away from her workplace and doing more active tasks around the office. Her awareness of the pedometer helped produce a lifestyle change.

Observable reminders have a place in our walk with Christ as well. (DM)

Magic-Marker Wisdom

The days are evil. Therefore do not be unwise. —Ephesians 5:16–17

A patient checked into a Florida hospital for a life-saving amputation. He awoke to find that the wrong foot had been removed. In the same hospital, another patient had surgery on the wrong knee.

Defenders of the healthcare system point out that such tragic cases of malpractice are like airline crashes—they are newsworthy because they are so rare. In that Florida hospital, however, officials responded with a plan to avoid such tragic mistakes in the future: Staffers now write "NO" with a black Magic Marker on the healthy limb. (MD)

Keep Laughing

A merry heart does good, like medicine, but a broken spirit dries the bones. —Proverbs 17:22

A judge ordered a fifty-four-year-old German man to stop bursting into laughter in the woods. Joachim Bahrenfeld, an accountant, was taken to court by one of several joggers who said they were disturbed by Bahrenfeld's deafening squeals of joy. He faced up to six months in jail if he was caught again. Bahrenfeld said he went to the woods to laugh nearly every day to relieve stress. "It is part of living for me," he said, "like eating, drinking, and breathing." He felt that a cheerful heart, expressed through hearty laughter, is important to his health and survival. (MW)

A Convenient Christianity

Whoever loses his life for My sake will find it. —Matthew 16:25

So many television programs, so little time to watch them. Apparently that's what our culture thinks, because now technology allows us to see an hour-long program in just six minutes or less! The Minisode Network has pruned episodes of popular series into shorter, more convenient packages for interested viewers. "The shows you love—only shorter" is how it's advertised. All to make our life more convenient.

Some have tried to make the Christian life more convenient. They choose to practice Christianity on Sunday only. They attend a religious service at whatever church makes them most comfortable. They give a small offering and are nice to fellow churchgoers—nothing that requires much effort on their part. That way they can have the rest of the week to themselves, to live as they please.

That would be a convenient Christianity. (AC)

Just for Show

All their works they do to be seen by men. —*Matthew 23:5*

An increasing number of antique leather-bound books are being purchased for their covers and not their content. Interior designers buy them by the linear yard and use them to create a warm, old-world atmosphere in the homes of affluent clients. Of prime importance is whether they match a room's decor. One wealthy businessman purchased 13,000 antique books he will never read just to create a library look in his renovated home. Those books are just for show. (DM)

Stay Home

Be doers of the word, and not hearers only. —*James 1:22*

A church member told his pastor that he was going to the Holy Land. He said that it was his intention to visit Mount Sinai. "In fact," he told the minister, "I plan to climb to the top of that mountain and read the Ten Commandments aloud when I get there."

Thinking this would please the pastor, he was surprised to hear, "You know, I can think of something even better than that."

The man responded, "You can, Pastor? And what might that be?"

"Instead of traveling thousands of miles to read the Ten Commandments on Mount Sinai, why not stay right here at home and keep them?" (RD)

True Winners

They [train] to obtain a perishable crown, but we for an imperishable crown. —*1 Corinthians 9:25*

After a baseball team from Georgia defeated a team from Japan in the Little League World Series, one reporter wrote: "The boys from Warner Robins left a lasting impression of their inner character for the world to see. They proved again, it's not whether you win or lose that counts. It is, how you play the game."

When the losing players broke down in tears, the winning team members stopped their victory celebration to console them. "I just hated to see them cry," said pitcher Kendall Scott, "and I just wanted to let them know that I care." Some referred to the moment as "sportsmanship at its best."

In sports, someone always loses. But when someone is won to Christ, the only loser is Satan. For Christians, true teamwork is not about defeating opponents; it's about recruiting them to join our team (1 Corinthians 9:19–22). (JAL)

CHRISTMAS

I WILL HONOR CHRISTMAS IN MY HEART, AND TRY
TO KEEP IT ALL THE YEAR. —CHARLES DICKENS

Hallelujah

I know that my Redeemer lives.   —Job 19:25

Composer George Frideric Handel was bankrupt when in 1741 a group of Dublin charities offered him a commission to write a musical work. It was for a benefit performance to raise funds to free men from a debtors' prison. He accepted that commission and worked tirelessly on the composition.

In just twenty-four days, Handel composed the well-known masterpiece *Messiah,* which contains "The Hallelujah Chorus." During that time he never left his home and often went without eating. At one point, a servant found him weeping over his evolving score. Recounting his experience, Handel wrote, "Whether I was in my body or out of my body as I wrote it I know not. God knows." Afterward he also said, "I did think I did see all heaven before me and the great God himself."

"The Hallelujah Chorus" stirs the soul whenever we hear it. (VG)

23

A Gift of Shelter

There was no room for them in the inn. —Luke 2:7

Life was tough for Datha and her family. At age thirty-nine, she had a heart attack and bypass surgery and learned that she had coronary artery disease. A year later, her fifteen-year-old daughter Heather became paralyzed as the result of a car accident. Datha quit her job to take care of Heather, and the bills started piling up. Soon they would be facing eviction. Datha was so angry with God that she stopped praying.

Then came Christmas Eve 2004. A young girl knocked on Datha's door. The girl wished her a Merry Christmas, gave her an envelope, and left quickly. Inside was a gift that would cover Datha's housing needs for the next year. The attached note read, "Please accept this gift in honor of the Man whose birthday we celebrate on this holy night. Long ago, His family also had a shelter problem." (AC)

Seeing at Christmas

God… commanded light to shine out of darkness. —2 Corinthians 4:6

During the Christmas season of 1879, an agnostic reporter in Boston saw three little girls standing in front of a store window full of toys. One of them was blind. He heard the other two describing the toys to their friend. He had never considered how difficult it was to explain to someone without sight what something looks like. That incident became the basis for a newspaper story.

Two weeks later the reporter attended a meeting held by Dwight L. Moody. His purpose was to catch the evangelist in an inconsistency. He was surprised when Moody used his account of the children to illustrate a truth. "Just as the blind girl couldn't visualize the toys," said Moody, "so an unsaved person can't see Christ in all His glory." (HVL)

CHURCH AND WORSHIP

THE PERFECT CHURCH SERVICE WOULD BE ONE WE WERE ALMOST UNAWARE OF. OUR ATTENTION WOULD HAVE BEEN ON GOD. —C. S. LEWIS

Hearing the Sermon Again

From that time Jesus began to preach and to say, "Repent, for the kingdom of heaven is at hand." —Matthew 4:17

A story is told about a man who preached an impressive sermon, seeking to be the pastor of a new church. Everybody loved it and voted for him to become their new pastor. They were a bit surprised, however, when he preached the same sermon his first Sunday there—and even more surprised when he preached it again the next week. After he preached the same sermon the third week in a row, the leaders met with him to find out what was going on. The pastor assured them, "I know what I'm doing. When you start living out this sermon, I'll go on to my next one." (JS)

Only a Rivet

The wisdom that is from above is first pure, then peaceable, gentle . . . without partiality and without hypocrisy. —James 3:17

Scientists have determined that faulty rivets may have caused the rapid sinking of the "unsinkable" HMS *Titanic*. According to researchers who recently examined parts recovered from the wreck, impure rivets made of wrought iron rather than steel caused the ship's hull to open like a zipper. The *Titanic* proves the foolishness of spending resources on fancy equipment and public promotion while neglecting the "ordinary" parts.

In a sense, churches are like ships, and many of their people are like rivets. (JAL)

Let's Party!

My soul longs, yes, even faints for the courts of the Lord. —Psalm 84:2

Tobias, who recently turned three, loves to go to church. He cries when he isn't able to attend. Each week when he arrives for the children's program of Bible stories, games, singing, and dinner, he runs into the building and enthusiastically announces to the leaders and other children: "Let's get this party started!" The Lord must smile at this child's excitement about being in what he thinks is God's house. (AC)

What Does God Like?

Be filled with the Spirit, speaking to one another in psalms and hymns and spiritual songs.   —Ephesians 5:18–19

We can all profit from a lesson a man learned on a business trip after attending a church service near his hotel. He talked with the pastor about how he had been blessed by the sermon, even though some of the worship time was not to his liking.

The pastor simply asked, "What was it you think God didn't like?" The man had the grace to reply, "I don't suppose there was anything He didn't like. I was talking about my own reaction. But worship isn't really about me, is it?" (VG)

"We Cut the Coal"

I commend to you Phoebe... for indeed she has been a helper of many and of myself also.   —Romans 16:1–2

Winston Churchill knew that people who work behind the scenes don't always get the credit they deserve. During World

War II, many of England's coal miners wanted to enlist and fight on the front lines. Churchill acknowledged their patriotism but reminded them of how valuable their work was to the cause of the war. "Some must stay in the pits," he said, "and others must stay in the army. Both are equally needed, and for both there is equal credit."

Looking ahead to when children would ask their parents what they did in the war, Churchill said, "One will say, 'I was a fighter pilot'; another will say, 'I was in the submarine service';... and you in your turn will say with equal pride and with equal right, 'We cut the coal.'" (DE)

Family Tie

The whole building, being fitted together, grows into a holy temple in the Lord. —Ephesians 2:21

An elderly man who visited an art gallery was deeply moved by a painting that portrayed Christ on the cross. It was so realistic in depicting the suffering of the Savior that his heart was filled with gratitude for the great price the Lord Jesus paid for his redemption. With tears trickling down his cheeks, he exclaimed, "Bless Him! I love Him! I love Him!"

Other visitors standing nearby wondered what the man was talking about. One person walked over and looked at the painting. Soon he too felt deep emotion welling up in his heart. Turning to the old man, he gave him a firm handshake and said, "So do I! I love Him too!" The scene was repeated as a third man and then a fourth walked over, gazed at the painting, and exclaimed, "I love Him too!" Although these men were from different churches, they felt a common bond because of their faith in Christ. (RD)

Train to Finish Strong

I discipline my body and bring it into subjection, lest, when I have preached to others, I myself should become disqualified.

—*1 Corinthians 9:27*

In 1924, Eric Liddell electrified the world by capturing an Olympic gold medal in the 400 meters—a race he was not expected to win. Liddell was the favorite at 100 meters, but he had withdrawn from that race after learning the qualifying heats would be on Sunday, a day he observed as one of worship and rest. Instead of lamenting his lost chance in the 100, he spent the next six months training for the 400—and set a new Olympic record.

Paul used a sports metaphor to emphasize the Christian's need for spiritual discipline. Liddell demonstrated it both as an athlete and later as a missionary to China. (DM)

Unsung

She has been a helper of many and of myself also.

—*Romans 16:2*

James Deitz has produced paintings of airplanes and their crews that are so realistic they look like photographs. His works hang in many aviation galleries in the United States, including the Smithsonian Institution.

One of the paintings by Deitz, titled *Unsung*, depicts a crew of four mechanics who are working on a dive-bomber. They are far below the flight deck of an aircraft carrier somewhere in the Pacific during World War II. The pale, serious-looking, grease-stained men are working tirelessly to get the plane ready to go back into battle.

We too may be performing unnoticed tasks as we support the church's mandate to spread the gospel and train believers. (DE)

COMFORT IN TRIALS

GRACE GROWS BEST IN WINTER. —SAMUEL RUTHERFORD

A Handful of Thorns

Give thanks to the Lord for His goodness, and for His wonderful works to the children of men! —Psalm 107:21

Jeremy Taylor was a seventeenth-century English cleric who was severely persecuted for his faith. But though his house was plundered, his family left destitute, and his property confiscated, he continued to count the blessings he could not lose.

He wrote: "They have not taken away my merry countenance, my cheerful spirit, and a good conscience; they have still left me with the providence of God, and all His promises... my hopes of Heaven, and my charity to them, too, and still I sleep and digest, I eat and drink, I read and meditate. And he that hath so many causes of joy, and so great, should never choose to sit down upon his little handful of thorns."

Although we may not be afflicted with the grievous difficulties that Jeremy Taylor endured, all of us face trials and troubles. (VG)

How to Walk

That He would grant you, according to the riches of His glory, to be strengthened with might through His Spirit in the inner man. —Ephesians 3:16

Dana and Rich went out for an afternoon bike ride expecting to come home refreshed. Instead, their lives were changed forever. As Rich rode down a hill, he lost control of his bike and crashed. His body was mangled, and he barely made it to the hospital alive.

Dana faithfully kept vigil by her husband's side. He couldn't feed himself, and he couldn't walk. One day, as the two of them sat under a shade tree outside the hospital, Rich turned to his wife and said, "Dana, I don't know if I'll ever walk again, but I'm learning to walk closer to Jesus, and that's what I really want."

Instead of shaking his fist at God, Rich reached out and grabbed His hand. (DB)

Count It All Joy

Blessed is the man who endures temptation; for when he has been approved, he will receive the crown of life. —*James 1:12*

A pastor placed this sign on his door: "If you have problems, come in and tell me all about them. If you don't have any problems, come in and tell me how you avoid them." (AL)

Rebuild!

Your people shall be my people, and your God, my God. —*Ruth 1:16*

On May 31, 1889, a massive rainstorm filled Lake Conemaugh in Pennsylvania until its dam finally gave way. A wall of water forty feet high traveling at forty miles per hour rushed down the valley toward the town of Johnstown. The torrent picked up buildings, animals, and human beings and sent them crashing down the spillway. When the lake had emptied itself, debris covered thirty acres, and 2,209 people were dead.

At first, stunned by the loss of property and loved ones, survivors felt hopeless. But later, community leaders gave speeches about how local industry and homes could be rebuilt. This acted like a healing balm, and the survivors energetically got to work. Johnstown was rebuilt and today is a thriving town with a population of approximately 28,000. (DF)

Dots and Doughnut Holes

Bless the Lord, O my soul, and forget not all His benefits. —Psalm 103:2

As a minister was addressing a group of men, he took a large piece of paper and made a black dot in the center of it. Then he held up the paper and asked them what they saw.

One person replied, "I see a black mark."

"Right," the preacher said. "What else?" Complete silence prevailed.

"I'm really surprised," the preacher commented. "You have completely overlooked the most important thing of all—the sheet of paper."

We are often distracted by small, dot-like disappointments, and we are prone to forget the innumerable blessings we receive from the Lord.

"As you travel down life's pathway, may this ever be your goal: Keep your eye upon the doughnut, and not upon the hole!" (RD)

COURAGE

COURAGE IS FEAR THAT HAS SAID ITS PRAYERS.
—DOROTHY BERNARD

Against the Flow

Do not be conformed to this world, but be transformed by the renewing of your mind.   *—Romans 12:2*

Two college students in Moorhead, Minnesota, painted a mural on the wall outside their dormitory room. According to *USA Today,* it showed a school of fish all swimming in the same direction except for a single fish heading the opposite way.

The one fish was intended to be the age-old symbol for Christ. Printed on the picture were the words, "Go against the flow." University officials, arguing that the mural might offend non-Christians, ordered the students to paint over it.

In obedience to our Master, we must be willing to go against the flow of society. (VG)

Beware!

Beware lest you also fall from your own steadfastness, being led away with the error of the wicked. —2 Peter 3:17

Daily life is hazardous to your health. That's the thesis of Laura Lee's book *100 Most Dangerous Things in Everyday Life and What You Can Do about Them.* It's a tongue-in-cheek look at the unnoticed threats in life, such as shopping carts (which annually cause 27,600 injuries in the U.S.) and dishwashers (which harm more than 7,000 Americans and 1,300 Britons each year). One reason for writing this book, the author says, was "to poke fun at the culture of fear."

In contrast, Jesus Christ calls His followers to a courageous lifestyle of faith in which our goal is not to avoid personal harm but to pursue the mission of God in our world. (DM)

Nick's Spirit

Neither this man nor his parents sinned, but that the works of God should be revealed in him. —John 9:3

If you didn't know him, you might think Nick Vujicic has everything going for him. Nick has never had a sore arm. He's never had knee problems. He's never smashed his finger in a door, stubbed his toe, or banged his shin against a table leg.

But that's because Nick doesn't have a shin. Or a toe. Or a finger. Or a knee. Or an arm. Nick was born with no arms and no legs. Before you begin to feel sorry for Nick, read his words: "God won't let anything happen to us in our life unless He has a good purpose for it all. I completely gave my life to Christ at the age of fifteen after reading John 9. Jesus said that the reason the man was born blind was 'so that the works of God may be revealed through him.'... I now see that glory revealed as He is using me just the way I am and in ways others can't be used." Nick travels the world to spread the gospel and love of Jesus.

Nick says, "If I can trust in God with my circumstances, then you can trust in God with your circumstances... The greatest joy of all is having Jesus Christ in my life and living the godly purpose He has for me." (DB)

The Reason and the Risk

I endure all things for the sake of the elect, that they also may obtain the salvation which is in Christ. —2 Timothy 2:10

It was the kind of moment that people have nightmares about. A tanker truck filled with 2,500 gallons of propane gas caught fire while parked at a fuel storage warehouse. The flames shot thirty to forty feet out of the back of the truck and quickly spread to a loading dock. Several large tanks nearby were in danger of exploding.

At that point, the plant manager, after helping to rescue the badly burned driver, jumped into the cab and drove the blazing truck away from the warehouse. His quick action and courage saved lives.

The apostle Paul also risked his life on behalf of others (2 Timothy 2:10). (MD)

Courage: Live It

God has not given us a spirit of fear, but of power. —2 Timothy 1:7

Courage is one thing you need if you want to get God's work done. That's what *ODB* author Dave Branon said when he spoke in a church service in Jamaica. He told the people that according to 2 Timothy 1:7, God did not give us a spirit of timidity but a spirit of power.

A couple of days later, he stood thirty-five feet above the water on the edge of the Caribbean Sea. Should he jump off the precipice into the waters below? The teenagers who were with him said, "Yes!" Most of them had already jumped. One told him, "Mr. Branon, if you don't jump, you can't preach about courage again." He knew that sometimes the courageous thing is not to go along with the crowd. But this time, he jumped.

Courage makes a good theory, but sometimes practicing it takes help and encouragement from others. (DB)

CREATION

THE MORE I STUDY NATURE, THE MORE I STAND AMAZED
AT THE WORK OF THE CREATOR. —LOUIS PASTEUR

Animal Necks

We have many members in one body, but all the members do not have the same function.   —Romans 12:4

Bison are made in such a way that their natural inclination is to look down; the design of their necks makes it difficult for them to look up. In contrast, giraffes are designed in a way that makes looking up easy; the way their necks were made makes it difficult for them to look down. Two creatures created by the same God but with distinctively different body parts and purposes. Giraffes eat leaves from branches above. Bison eat grass from the field below. God provides food for both, and neither has to become like the other to eat. (JAL)

How Great Is Our God

Can you bind the cluster of the Pleiades, or loose the belt of Orion?
—Job 38:31

A team of astronomers from the University of Minnesota says it has found a giant hole in the universe. The void they've discovered is in a region of sky southwest of Orion. The mysterious empty place has no galaxies, stars, or even dark matter. One of the astronomers said that the hole in the heavens is a billion light-years across.

Who can relate to the magnitude of such emptiness?

Think of what the Lord did with Job. He drew His suffering servant's attention to the same part of the night sky. Using the region of the constellation Orion along with the wonders of the weather and the natural world, the Lord brought Job to the end of his reasonings and arguments (Job 38:31; 42:5–6). (MD)

Ignoring the Creator

Since the creation of the world His invisible attributes are clearly seen.
—Romans 1:20

A man wearing jeans, a T-shirt, and a baseball cap positioned himself against a wall beside a trashcan at the L'Enfant Plaza station in Washington, DC. He pulled out a violin and began to play. In the next forty-three minutes, as he performed six classical pieces, 1,097 people passed by, ignoring him.

No one knew it, but the man playing outside the Metro was Joshua Bell, one of the finest classical musicians in the world, playing some of the most elegant music ever written on a $3.5 million Stradivarius. But no crowd gathered for the virtuoso. "It was a strange feeling, that people were actually ... ignoring me," said Bell.

God also knows what if feels like to be ignored. (MW)

More Than We Imagine

We are children of God; and it has not yet been revealed what we shall be, but we know that when He is revealed, we shall be like Him.   —1 John 3:2

For decades, artists have painted scenes of the universe based on a combination of scientific information and their own imaginations. But photographs from robotic space probes and the Hubble Space Telescope have redefined these artists' view of reality. In a *Los Angeles Times* article, space artist Don Dixon said the first pictures of Jupiter's moons Io and Europa "turned out to be much more exotic than anybody imagined." Dixon now considers 70 percent of his space paintings to be "dated concepts" because reality has become more awesome than imagination. (DM)

Mount St. Helens Syndrome

The longsuffering of our Lord is salvation.   —2 Peter 3:15

On March 20, 1980, Mount St. Helens in Washington, a supposedly dormant volcano, began to quake and rumble. The local population was evacuated to a "safe" distance eight miles away. Later, the side of the mountain began to bulge. Scientists were not alarmed because past research of volcanoes indicated that they never blew sideways.

Then on May 18 the side of Mount St. Helens exploded, shooting tons of debris downhill at the speed of 150 miles per hour. A minute later, the volcano exploded upward with the equivalent power of 500 atomic bombs, killing 57 people and devastating 230 square miles of forest.

The scientists had assumed that natural events would continue as before. But they were wrong.

The Bible tells us that many mistakenly place their confidence in the wrong things. The good news is that our true "safety" is the salvation provided by faith in Jesus Christ. (DF)

Beyond Amazing

The heavens are the work of Your hands. —Psalm 102:25

In 1977 the United States launched a rocket into space. On board was a small craft called Voyager I, a probe that was jettisoned into space to explore the planets. After Voyager was done sending back photos and data from the planet Jupiter and its neighbors, it didn't stop working. It just kept going.

Today, that tiny vehicle is still going—traveling at a speed of over 38,000 miles per hour. In the year 2020 it will be more than ten billion miles from the sun. That's mind-boggling! Brilliant scientists have sent a ship to the edge of our solar system—and beyond.

It's astounding. It's amazing. But it's absolutely puny when compared with what God has done. (DB)

We Don't Need You

What injustice have your fathers found in Me,
That they have gone far from Me,
Have followed idols,
And have become idolaters?
—Jeremiah 2:5

A story is told about a group of scientists who decided that humans could do without God. So one of them looked up to God and said, "We've decided that we no longer need you. We have enough wisdom to clone people and do many miraculous things."

God listened patiently and then said, "Very well, let's have a man-making contest. We'll do it just like I did back in the old days with Adam."

The scientists agreed, and one of them bent down and picked up a handful of dirt. God looked at him and said, "No! You have to make your own dirt!" (AC)

Is Evolution a Fact?

By faith we understand that the worlds were framed by the word of God. —*Hebrews 11:3*

The theory of evolution is not without its problems. One scientist says this about life starting on its own: "Amino acids would have to be arranged in an exact sequence to form a protein... just like the letters in a sentence. Mere laws of chemistry and physics cannot do that. The probability of a protein forming by chance would be 10^{64} [10 with 64 zeros after it] to 1!"

Many people assume the theory of evolution to be true. But can it be scientifically proven? Something is considered scientifically true only if it can be repeatedly verified under laboratory conditions. The claim that life sprang up on its own out of a long impersonal process cannot pass this test of truth. (DF)

CULTURE

WHATEVER MAKES MEN GOOD CHRISTIANS MAKES THEM GOOD CITIZENS. —DANIEL WEBSTER

Cross Fee

God forbid that I should boast except in the cross of our Lord Jesus Christ. —*Galatians 6:14*

In April 2006 a Methodist church in the city of Dudley, England, found out that it would have to pay a fee to put a cross on its new building. Yes, a fee was required because under British law the cross is an advertisement. It proclaims to the world, whether on a person or a building, that the bloodstained cross of Calvary is our only hope of forgiveness and salvation. (VG)

January Blues

Be of good cheer! It is I; do not be afraid. —Matthew 14:27

Scientists in the UK have calculated that the most depressing day of the year comes in the third week of January. Winter days are dark and cold, holiday excitement has worn off just as Christmas debts are coming due, and New Year's resolutions have all been broken. The celebrations, gift-giving, and good intentions that once made us feel happy now press us down and leave us feeling hopeless. (JAL)

Get Involved

Inasmuch as you did it to one of the least of these My brethren, you did it to Me. —Matthew 25:40

While working for the U.S. Justice Department, Gary Haugen discovered a big problem. *Someone needs to do something about this,* he thought. He looked around for someone who could take on the injustice and abuse of authority he had uncovered. But then he realized that God was looking at him. So in 1997 Haugen founded International Justice Mission to rescue victims of violence, sexual exploitation, slavery, and oppression. (JAL)

Brighten Up

Be tenderhearted, be courteous. —1 Peter 3:8

British and American computer scientists have created artwork that changes according to how the viewer feels. The computer program analyzes the position and shape of the mouth, the angle of the brows, the openness of the eyes, and five other facial features to determine the viewer's emotional state. The artwork then alters, based on the viewer's mood. If joy is seen on the face, the artwork will show up in bright colors. If there's a scowl, the image will become dark and somber. (AC)

Get a Horse!

Ask for the old paths,
where the good way is,
And walk in it;
Then you will find rest for your souls.
—Jeremiah 6:16

On a cold winter day in Michigan, a woman in labor was being rushed to the hospital when the unthinkable happened. The ambulance slid off an icy road into a ditch. A passing four-wheel drive truck stopped and tried to haul the emergency vehicle out but couldn't get a grip on it.

That's when real help arrived. An Amish man driving a two-horse team stopped to offer help. He told the ambulance service that the horses' shoes had been sharpened so they would bite into the ice. Once he hooked up the horses to the ambulance, they walked it right out of the ditch. (MD)

DEATH

DEATH IS THE GOLDEN KEY THAT OPENS THE PALACE OF ETERNITY. — JOHN MILTON

Last Words

At my first defense no one stood with me, but all forsook me. May it not be charged against them.   *—2 Timothy 4:16*

Just days before his death, Gandhi wrote, "All about me is darkness; I am praying for light." By contrast, evangelist D. L. Moody's last recorded words were, "This is my triumph; this my coronation day! It is glorious!" In both cases, their last words were significant expressions of their perspectives on life, death, and everything in between. (BC)

The Heaven File

We who are alive and remain shall be caught up together with them in the clouds to meet the Lord in the air. —1 Thessalonians 4:17

ODB author David McCasland says his wife, Luann, has a folder she calls her "heaven file." It contains articles, obituaries, and photos, along with cards from the memorial services of family and friends. She keeps them, not as a sad reminder of people she has loved and lost, but in anticipation of a future glad reunion with them in heaven. (DM)

Able to Forget?

I thank my God upon every remembrance of you.
—Philippians 1:3

On a cold, dreary November day, *ODB* author Bill Crowder recounts, he attended the funeral of a friend. During the eulogy, the widow began to sob loudly. At that point, the pastor spoke odd words meant to comfort: "That's okay. Someday you'll be able to forget."

Able to forget? The widow's expression made it clear that she had no desire to forget. (BC)

New Bodies

Jesus, the author and finisher of our faith, who for the joy that was set before Him endured the cross. —Hebrews 12:2

In 1728, a young Ben Franklin composed his own tombstone epitaph:

"The body of B. Franklin, printer, like the cover of an old book, its contents worn out, and stript of its lettering and gilding, lies here, food for worms. Yet the work shall

41

not be lost; for it will as he believ'd appear once more, in a new & more beautiful edition, corrected and amended by the Author."

In this epitaph, the wry wit of Franklin, the colonial Renaissance man, rings true to the biblical view of resurrection. The bodies we now possess are prone to aging, physical decline, and ultimately death. But the resurrection of Jesus Christ holds within it the promise of a new supernatural body raised in glory. The apostle Paul tells us, "The body is sown in corruption, it is raised in incorruption. It is sown in dishonor, it is raised in glory. It is sown in weakness, it is raised in power" (1 Corinthians 15:42–43). (DF)

For Whom the Bell Tolls

Death is swallowed up in victory. O Death, where is your sting?
—1 Corinthians 15:54–55

In seventeenth-century England, church bells tolled out the news of what was taking place in a parish. They announced not only religious services but also weddings and funerals.

So when John Donne, author and dean of St. Paul's Cathedral, lay desperately sick with the plague that was killing people in London by the thousands, he could hear the bells announce death after death. Writing down his thoughts in the devotional diary that became a classic, Donne urged his readers, "Never send to know for whom the bell tolls. It tolls for thee." (VG)

What's the Point?

Fear God and keep His commandments, for this is man's all.
—Ecclesiastes 12:13

Scientists once thought that the vertebrate with the shortest life span was the turquoise killifish. This small fish lives in seasonal rain pools in equatorial Africa and must complete its life cycle in twelve weeks, before the pools disappear.

But researchers from James Cook University in Australia have now found that the pygmy goby has an even shorter life span. It lives fast and dies young. This tiny fish lives in coral reefs for an average of fifty-nine days. Its rapid reproductive cycle is designed to help it avoid extinction.

What's the point of a life that goes so fast and ends so quickly? It's a question asked and answered by one of the wisest men who ever lived: Significance is not found in the number of our days, but in what our eternal God says about how we have used them. (MD)

Joy List

These things I have spoken to you, that My joy may remain in you, and that your joy may be full. —John 15:11

Writer C. W. Metcalf was working as a hospice volunteer when he met thirteen-year-old Chuck, who was terminally ill. One day Chuck gave Metcalf half a dozen sheets of paper with writing on both sides and said, "I want you to give this to my mom and dad after I die. It's a list of all the fun we had, all the times we laughed." Metcalf was amazed that this young boy on the verge of death was thinking about the well-being of others.

Metcalf delivered the list. Years later, he decided to make a list of his own. Surprisingly, he found it difficult at first to compile his "joy list." But as he began looking each day for the moments of laughter, satisfaction, and joy, his list began to grow. (DM)

How Would You Answer?

The Lord Himself will descend from heaven with a shout... And the dead in Christ will rise first. —1 Thessalonians 4:16

Sir Norman Anderson was invited to give a television talk on the evidence for Christ's resurrection, a subject that he had written much about. When his son died of cancer, the program producers offered to cancel his participation, saying, "You can't speak about the resurrection when you've just lost a son."

But Anderson said, "I want to speak about it now even more." And so, sad in heart but with great assurance, he spoke of Christ's resurrection, and ours as believers. (JY)

FACTS AND TRIVIA

I HAVE NO SPECIAL TALENTS. I AM ONLY PASSIONATELY CURIOUS. —ALBERT EINSTEIN

Just Add Time

The things that you have heard from me... commit these to faithful men who will be able to teach others also. —2 Timothy 2:2

A man who played double bass in the Mexico City Philharmonic told *ODB* author David McCasland that the finest instruments are made of wood that has been allowed to age naturally to remove the moisture. "You must age the wood for eighty years, then play the instrument for eighty years before it reaches its best sound," Luis Antonio Rojas said to McCasland. "A craftsman must use wood cut and aged by someone else, and he will never see any instrument reach its peak during his own lifetime." (DM)

Time Well Spent

Lord, make me to know my end, and what is the measure of my days, that I may know how frail I am. —Psalm 39:4

How would you like to spend two years making phone calls to people who aren't home? Sound absurd? According to one time management study, that's how much time the average person spends in a lifetime trying to return calls to people who never seem to be in. Not only that, we spend six months waiting for the traffic light to turn green and another eight months reading junk mail. (DB)

Finding the Truth

As you therefore have received Christ ... so walk in Him, rooted and built up in Him and established in the faith.   —Colossians 2:6–7

How would you answer the following questions:

1. Did Jesus ever sin?
2. Was Jesus resurrected?
3. Do all religions teach the same basic ideas?

According to George Barna and Mark Hatch in their book *Boiling Point*, many people who call themselves Christians have a hard time with questions like these. When Barna and Hatch surveyed professing believers, one-fourth said Jesus committed sins, one-third said He did not rise from the dead, and one-third said all religions are basically the same. (DB)

Why We Have Value

As many as received Him, to them He gave the right to become children of God.   —John 1:12

In a commencement address to a graduating class at the University of Miami, columnist George Will gave some statistics that help to diminish our sense of self-importance. He pointed out that "the sun around which Earth orbits is one of perhaps 400 billion stars in the Milky Way, which is a piddling galaxy next door to nothing much." He added, "There are perhaps forty billion galaxies in the still-unfolding universe. If all the stars in the universe were only the size of the head of a pin, they still would fill Miami's Orange Bowl to overflowing more than three billion times."

There is a plus side to all that overwhelming data. The God who created and sustains our star-studded cosmos in its incomprehensible vastness loves us. (VG)

Prisoners of Sin

The Scripture has confined all under sin, that the promise by faith in Jesus Christ might be given to those who believe.

—*Galatians 3:22*

A 2008 report from the United Nations Office on Drugs and Crime said, "At any given time there are more than ten million people imprisoned worldwide." Since some prisoners are being released while new ones are being sentenced every day, there are more than thirty million total prisoners worldwide each year. Statistics like these have caused many people to work for prison reform and a reexamination of sentencing laws.

From a spiritual perspective, the Bible offers an even more staggering statistic: "The Scripture declares that the whole world is a prisoner of sin" (Galatians 3:22 NIV). (DM)

My Seventh Wife

Even though our outward man is perishing, yet the inward man is being renewed day by day.   —*2 Corinthians 4:16*

Science tells us that we get a new body every seven years, Dr. M. R. De Haan wrote. The cells of our body are used up in the process of metabolism, resulting in a complete change of tissue every seven years. The body may change, but the soul and the spirit remain the same. Therefore, concluded Dr, De Haan about his marriage to Priscilla, "In our forty-four years of married life, I've had seven wives, but she's the same wonderful one." (MRD)

Bearing Fruit

By this My Father is glorified, that you bear much fruit.

—*John 15:8*

A few years ago, the Museum of Science and Industry in Chicago had a fascinating display. It showed a checkerboard with one grain of wheat on the first square, two on the second, four on the third, then eight, sixteen, thirty-two, sixty-four, and so on until they could no longer fit the seeds on the square. Then it asked the question, "At this rate of doubling each successive square, how much would you have on the checkerboard by the sixty-fourth square?"

You could punch a button at the bottom of the display to find out. The answer? "Nine sextillion—enough grain to cover the entire subcontinent of India fifty feet deep." Incredible! (DE)

FAITH

FAITH SEES THE INVISIBLE, BELIEVES THE UNBELIEVABLE, AND RECEIVES THE IMPOSSIBLE. —CORRIE TEN BOOM

Desert Pete

The word which they heard did not profit them, not being mixed with faith. —*Hebrews 4:2*

In the 1960s, the Kingston Trio released a song called "Desert Pete." The ballad tells of a thirsty cowboy who is crossing the desert and finds a hand pump. Next to it, Desert Pete has left a note urging travelers not to drink from the jar hidden there but to use its contents to prime the pump.

The cowboy resists the temptation to drink and uses the water as the note instructs. In reward for his obedience, he receives an abundance of cold, satisfying water. Had he not acted in faith, believing what Desert Pete wrote in his note, the cowboy would have had only a jar of unsatisfying, warm water to drink.

This reminds me of Israel's journey through the wilderness. (DF)

The Leap

By faith Abraham obeyed when he was called to go out.
—Hebrews 11:8

During a baseball game in the summer of 2006, Boston Red Sox centerfielder Coco Crisp made a spectacular play. David Wright of the New York Mets hit a ball toward left centerfield. The ball was moving away from Crisp as he raced after it. Just as it began to fall to the ground, Crisp dove headlong toward it. With his body flying through the air, he stretched his gloved hand as far as possible—and caught the ball. Some called it the best catch they had ever seen.

What were his thoughts as the ball sliced through the air? Crisp said, "I didn't think I could get there. I decided to go for it. I took a leap of faith." (DB)

Farsighted Faith

For I know that my Redeemer lives,
And He shall stand at last on the earth;
And after my skin is destroyed, this I know,
That in my flesh I shall see God.
—Job 19:25–26

Faith looks beyond this life to eternity. A thirty-two-year-old mother who had leukemia didn't like to think of the possibility of leaving behind her husband and small children. She prayed for a remission or a cure. Her loved ones and friends prayed with her. Nobody knew what God would do. Yet she was full of faith. She testified that she could be happy because she knew that nothing really bad could happen to her. She saw beyond death to the resurrection of the body, reunion with her loved ones, and a home in heaven. Hers was not a shortsighted idealism but a farsighted faith. (HVL)

Small Faith in a Big God

If you have faith as a mustard seed, you will say to this mountain,
"Move from here to there," and it will move. —Matthew 17:20

Faith—we all wish we had more of it, especially when facing mountainous problems. Yet most of us are well practiced in faith. We sit down in chairs without checking them out; we use microwave ovens without analyzing how they work; we put keys in doors and expect them to open. We don't go around moaning, "If only I had more faith in chairs, in microwaves, in keys." We depend on these objects because we see them as reliable—not because we've worked up great feelings of confidence.

Jesus didn't say to His disciples, "Have more faith in God." He simply said, "Have faith in God" (Mark 11:22). (JY)

"Mower" Faith

O Lord God of my master Abraham, please give me success this day.
—Genesis 24:12

The fifth-grader watched her father struggling under the hot sun to cut the grass on the family's sizable yard. When he was finally done, she said to him, "Daddy, I wish we had a riding lawn mower. I'm going to buy you one." She did more than make what seemed like an impossible promise. She began praying for a riding mower for her dad. And she began doing odd jobs to earn money.

Finally the girl had saved up fifty dollars, but everyone knew that wasn't enough. Then one day she and her mom saw a riding mower that was for sale. When they took a closer look at the sign, they couldn't believe their eyes: It was for sale for fifty dollars. And the mower worked!

In Genesis 24, we read the account of Abraham's servant seeking a bride for Isaac. He had the difficult task of finding a woman from a family hundreds of miles away. And she had to be willing to return with him to Canaan. He prayed specifically, did everything he could, and waited on the Lord.

Two seemingly impossible requests. Two faithful believers in prayer and action. It's a formula for great results. (DB)

FAMILY

A MAN TRAVELS THE WORLD OVER IN SEARCH OF
WHAT HE NEEDS, AND RETURNS HOME TO FIND IT.
—GEORGE MOORE

God's Gift

Mephibosheth... shall eat at my table like one of the king's sons.
—*2 Samuel 9:11*

A British factory worker and his wife were excited when, after many years of marriage, they discovered they were going to have their first child. According to author Jill Briscoe, who told this story, the man eagerly told his fellow workers that God had answered his prayers. But they made fun of him for asking God for a child.

When the baby was born, he was diagnosed with Down syndrome. As the father made his way to work for the first time after the birth, he wondered how to face his co-workers. "God, please give me wisdom," he prayed. Just as he feared, some mocked, "So, God gave you this child!" The new father stood for a long time, silently asking God for help. At last he said, "I'm glad the Lord gave this child to me and not to you." (DB)

Value Test

Why do you call Me "Lord, Lord," and not do the things which I say?
—*Luke 6:46*

One business executive, who said his five-year-old daughter was the most important part of his life, realized that he usually went to work before she got up in the morning and often returned home after she was in bed at night. So to spend time with her, he took her to work with him one Saturday. After looking around his office, she asked, "Daddy, is this where you live?" He may have acknowledged that his daughter was important, but his behavior revealed what he truly valued. (DM)

The Legacy

I have no greater joy than to hear that my children walk in truth.
—3 John 1:4

Her writing career spanned three decades, from the mid-1960s through the mid-1990s. She wrote twelve books and received sixteen honorary doctorate degrees. But three years before she died of cancer in 1996, popular humorist Erma Bombeck told an ABC TV interviewer that no matter how many columns she had written, her legacy would be her three children. "If I did a bad job with them," she said, "then everything else [I] do isn't very important."

Bombeck had riches and fame and the goodwill of millions of readers, but she realized that her top priority was taking care of her children. (DB)

Whose Fault?

Live joyfully with the wife whom you love all the days of your vain life which He has given you under the sun.   —Ecclesiastes 9:9

A man went to his pastor for counseling. In his hands were pages of complaints against his wife. After hours of uninterrupted listening, the pastor couldn't help but ask, "If she is that bad, why did you marry her?" Immediately the man shot back, "She wasn't like this at first!" The pastor, unable to hold back his thoughts, asked, "So, are you saying that she is like this because she's been married to you?" (AL)

Too Late

I sought the Lord, and He heard me.   —Psalm 34:4

Jane Welsh, secretary to Scottish essayist Thomas Carlyle (1795–1881), married him and devoted her life to him and his work. He loved her deeply but was so busy with his writing and speaking that he often neglected her. Some time into their marriage, she became ill and suddenly died.

After the funeral, Carlyle went to Jane's room and looked at her diary. He found these words she had written about him: "Yesterday he spent an hour with me and it was like heaven. I love him so." On another day, she wrote, "I have listened all day to hear his steps in the hall, but now it is late. I guess he will not come today." He wept brokenly, realizing his neglect of her and her desire just to talk with him.

God listens attentively for our call, our cry, our prayer. How often does He wait in vain? (DE)

Maxwell's House

That they may arise and declare [God's law] to their children, that they may set their hope in God. —Psalm 78:6–7

In nineteenth-century Scotland, a young mother observed and encouraged her three-year-old son's inquisitive nature. It seemed he was curious about everything that moved or made a noise. James Clerk Maxwell would carry his boyhood wonder with him into a remarkable career in science. He went on to do groundbreaking work in electricity and magnetism. Years later, Albert Einstein would say of Maxwell's work that it was "the most fruitful that physics has experienced since the time of Newton."

From early childhood, religion touched all aspects of Maxwell's life. As a committed Christian, he prayed: "Teach us to study the works of Thy hands... and strengthen our reason for Thy service." The boyhood cultivation of Maxwell's spiritual life and curiosity resulted in a lifetime of using science in service to the Creator. (DF)

My Prince

Husbands, love your wives. —Ephesians 5:25

People around the world reacted with shock in September 2006 when news broke that Steve Irwin, the "Crocodile Hunter," had died. His enthusiasm for life and for God's creatures was contagious, making him a favorite personality worldwide.

When his wife Terri was interviewed shortly after Steve's death, her love for him was obvious as she said through her tears, "I've lost my prince." What a loving way to memorialize her husband! She saw him as her prince and her best friend.

The husband-wife relationship is often viewed today as anything but the tender one Terri and Steve must have shared. (DB)

The Dead Sea Squirrels

You shall teach them diligently to your children.

—*Deuteronomy 6:7*

ODB author Dennis Fisher tells that his family was excited to visit the Dead Sea Scrolls exhibit that was coming to town all the way from Israel. These ancient copies of the Old Testament provide evidence that the Bible has remained accurate over the centuries. Dennis's nephew Daniel was so elated about this outing that he told his schoolmates, "Our family is going to see 'the Dead Sea squirrels!'"

"We all laughed when we heard his misquote," Dennis said. "His little ears had turned a word he had never heard (scrolls) into a word he did know (squirrels). And in his childlike enthusiasm, he also knew that the family was going to see something wonderful!"

Daniel's excitement underscores an important spiritual aspect of parenting. Values are transmitted to our children not only by the things we say but also by the emotions we convey. (DF)

Dad's Hat

Honor your father.　　　　　　　　　—*Ephesians 6:2*

Amid the celebration, there was tragedy. It was the opening ceremonies of the 1992 Summer Olympic Games in Barcelona. One by one the teams entered the stadium and paraded around the track to the cheers of 65,000 people. But in one section of

Olympic Stadium shock and sadness fell as Peter Karnaugh, father of United States swimmer Ron Karnaugh, was stricken with a fatal heart attack.

Five days later, Ron showed up for his race wearing his dad's hat, which he carefully set aside before his competition began. Why the hat? It was the swimmer's tribute to his dad, whom he described as "my best friend." The hat was one his dad had worn when they went fishing and did other things together. Wearing the hat was Ron's way of honoring his dad for standing beside him, encouraging him, and guiding him. When Ron dove into the water, he did so without his dad's presence but inspired by his memory. (DB)

Keep the Romance

Keep yourselves in the love of God.   —Jude 21

The great American statesman and lawyer William Jennings Bryan (1860–1925) was having his portrait painted. The artist asked, "Why do you wear your hair over your ears?"

Bryan responded, "There is a romance connected with that. When I began courting Mrs. Bryan, she objected to the way my ears stood out. So, to please her, I let my hair grow to cover them."

"That was many years ago," the artist said. "Why don't you have your hair cut now?"

"Because," Bryan winked, "the romance is still going on." (DE)

FEAR

WORRY GIVES A SMALL THING A BIG SHADOW.
—SWEDISH PROVERB

Always Awake

I will both lie down in peace, and sleep; for You alone, O Lord, make me dwell in safety. —*Psalm 4:8*

A mother and her four-year-old daughter were preparing for bed. The child was afraid of the dark. When the lights were turned off, the girl noticed the moon shining through the window. "Mommy," she asked, "is that God's light up there?"

"Yes, it is," came the reply.

Soon another question: "Will He put it out and go to sleep too?"

"Oh no, He never goes to sleep."

After a few silent moments, the little girl said, "As long as God is awake, I'm not scared." Realizing that the Lord would be watching over her, the reassured child soon fell into a peaceful sleep. (PVG)

Afraid to Be Afraid

Whenever I am afraid, I will trust in You. —*Psalm 56:3*

A young woman was waiting for a bus in a crime-ridden area when a rookie policeman approached her and asked, "Do you want me to wait with you?"

"That's not necessary," she replied. "I'm not afraid."

"Well, I am," he grinned. "Would you mind waiting with me?"

Like that policeman, we as Christians must be willing to admit that sometimes we become fearful. (DD)

Is Fear Healthy?

The fear of the Lord is the instruction of wisdom. —Proverbs 15:33

During a severe thunderstorm, a mother tucked her child into bed and turned off the light. Frightened by the tempest, he asked, "Mommy, will you sleep with me?"

Hugging him, she replied, "I can't, dear. I have to sleep with Daddy."

Stepping out of the room, she heard, "That big sissy!" (AL)

Coping with Fear

As for me, I trust in You, O Lord. —Psalm 31:14

Many people are afraid of flying. The thought of being airborne fills them with anxiety. For that reason the American Phobic Society recommends these techniques for coping with the fear of flying:

- Avoid sugar and caffeine before and during a flight.
- Lean back at takeoff; let your muscles go limp.
- Rate your anxiety on a scale from 1 to 10. Think positive thoughts; note how much your fear decreases.
- Breathe deeply; close your eyes; stretch your arms.
- Wear a rubber band on your wrist and snap it to break unpleasant thoughts.

These are five good suggestions. But here's a sixth that works with all kinds of fear. In fact, it's the most important of all: Put your trust in God. (DE)

FORGIVENESS

FORGIVENESS DOES NOT CHANGE THE PAST, BUT IT DOES ENLARGE THE FUTURE. —PAUL BOESE

God's Way

Blessed is he whose transgression is forgiven, whose sin is covered.
—Psalm 32:1

A little boy had just been tucked into bed by his mother, who was waiting to hear his prayers. But he had been naughty that day, and now it was bothering him. So he said, "Mama, I wish you'd go now and leave me alone. I want to pray by myself."

Sensing that something was wrong, she asked, "Bobby, is there anything you ought to tell me?"

"No, Mommy," he replied. "You would just scold me, but God will forgive me and forget about it." (RD)

They Never Meet

You have cast all my sins behind Your back.   —Isaiah 38:17

Did you know that the farthest point east and the farthest point west in the United States are both in Alaska? It's a geographical trick, actually. Pochnoi Point in the Aleutians is as far west as you can go and still be in the U.S. But if you travel a few miles farther west, you'll end up at Alaska's Amatignak Island. Because that spot is west of the 180th meridian separating the Eastern and Western Hemispheres, it is technically east of the rest of the U.S.

But you'll never find a spot where east and west are actually next to each other. In going west, you never "find" east. East goes on forever. West goes on forever. They never meet. You can't get farther from something than that.

What difference does this make? Just this: When you read in Scripture that your forgiven sins are separated from you "as far as the east is from the west" (Psalm 103:12), you are assured that they are an immeasurable distance away—gone forever. (DB)

Erev Yom Kippur

First be reconciled to your brother, and then come and offer your gift. —Matthew 5:24

In Judaism, the holiest day of the year is Yom Kippur, the Day of Atonement. On that day, the nation seeks God's forgiveness for sins both personal and national.

What is interesting, however, is the day before Yom Kippur, known as Erev Yom Kippur. It represents a person's last opportunity to seek forgiveness from other people before Yom Kippur begins. This is important because, in Jewish thought, you must seek forgiveness from other people before you can seek the forgiveness of God. (BC)

Cleaning Out the Files

Forgetting those things which are behind... I press toward the goal for the prize of the upward call of God in Christ Jesus. —Philippians 3:13–14

A certain businessman was notorious for saving almost everything that came across his desk, especially correspondence. Consequently, the files in his office were bulging. One day his secretary asked if she might dispose of all the old, useless material. The man was reluctant but finally said, "Well, all right, but be sure you make a copy of everything before you throw it away."

That's the way some Christians handle their sins. They know that Jesus paid the penalty, but somehow they can't let go of the guilt. (DD)

Lifting a Burden

Do not therefore be grieved or angry with yourselves because you sold me. —*Genesis 45:5*

It was the last weekend of the 1964 baseball season. Bill Valentine was umpiring a game between the Detroit Tigers and the New York Yankees.

Dave Wickersham was pitching for Detroit, and he had nineteen victories for the season. One more would be a sign of stardom. But it wasn't to be.

After a close play, Wickersham tapped the umpire on the shoulder to ask for a time-out. Touching an umpire is against the rules, so Valentine tossed Wickersham from the game—depriving him of his chance for a twenty-win season.

For the next thirty-nine years, Valentine lived with a gnawing regret for booting the pitcher in that split-second decision. But he doesn't carry that regret anymore. After all that time, Wickersham wrote the umpire a note, telling him he was right in his decision and that he held no hard feelings. That note lifted a weight from Valentine's shoulders. (DB)

FRIENDSHIP

A TRUE FRIEND REACHES FOR YOUR HAND AND
TOUCHES YOUR HEART. —AUTHOR UNKNOWN

Making Chums

A friend loves at all times, and a brother is born for adversity. —*Proverbs 17:17*

In nineteenth-century England, debtors' prison housed those unfortunate souls who couldn't pay their bills. New prisoners were escorted to the "chummage," a prison dormitory. Since the people were not there for violent crimes, a spirit of trust and camaraderie soon developed. They played games together and had plenty to eat. Some were even allowed private rooms.

In time, the prisoners began to refer to each other as "chums." Later, the word caught on outside the prison walls and took on the meaning of "a cordial friend." (DF)

——————— International Friendship ———————

We give thanks to the God and Father of our Lord Jesus Christ, praying always for you.   —Colossians 1:3

In 1947, Nadia from Bulgaria and Millicent from the United States became pen pals. For years they swapped photos, school experiences, and dreams. Then their letters stopped when Bulgarian government policy banned personal contact with the West.

After many years of political upheaval and change, Millicent, on a whim, sent a letter to the last address she had for Nadia. To their delight, the letter got through. Before long, they discovered that both had married doctors and both collected seashells. Forty-eight years after their first letter, the two friends finally met at Miami International Airport, where Millicent exclaimed, "Nadia! I would know you anywhere!"

Like Nadia and Millicent's letters, the letters of the apostle Paul overflow with affection and gratitude for his friends. (MD)

——————— A New Friend ———————

I have called you friends, for all things that I heard from My Father I have made known to you.   —John 15:15

Cornerstone University president and *ODB* writer Joe Stowell tells this story.

While flying from Europe back to the U.S., I found myself sitting next to a little girl who never stopped talking from the moment she sat down. She told me the history of her family and all about her puppy, which was in the hold of the plane. She pointed excitedly to everything around us, "Look at this! Look at that!" I couldn't help but think that eight hours of this could make for a very long flight!

We chatted for a while until she suddenly got quiet. She pulled her blanket up around her, so I thought maybe she was going to doze off. I quickly took advantage of the break and reached for the nearest magazine. But before I could open it, I felt a little elbow in my side. I looked down at her, and she threw out her little hand and said, "Hey, Joe, wanna be friends?"

My heart melted. "Sure," I said, "let's be friends." (JS)

Rebuke from a Friend

Faithful are the wounds of a friend, but the kisses of an enemy are deceitful. —Proverbs 27:6

"Never will I forget the rebuke I received from a friend when I was seventeen," recalled *ODB* writer Herb Vander Lugt. "My friend walked into the back of the butcher shop where I worked and saw me laughing at an indecent cartoon. He said he had admired my Christian character and was surprised that I would laugh at something sinful and degrading. Instantly a wave of embarrassment swept over me. I shamefully admitted that I had sinned." (HVL)

GIVING

No one has ever become poor by giving. —Anne Frank

I Dare You

I have hoped in Your ordinances. So shall I keep Your law continually. —Psalm 119:43–44

The story is told about a small church that was having a reunion. A former member who attended the celebration had become a millionaire. When he testified about how God had blessed him over the years, he related an incident from his childhood.

He said that when he earned his first dollar as a boy, he decided to keep it for the rest of his life. But then a guest missionary preached about the urgent need on the mission field. He struggled about giving his dollar. "The Lord won, however," the man said. Then, with a sense of pride he added, "I put my treasured dollar in the offering basket. And I am convinced that the reason God has blessed me so much is that when I was a little boy I gave Him everything I possessed."

The congregation was awestruck by the testimony—until an elderly woman in the front row piped up, "I dare you to do it again!" (DE)

A Loan to the Lord

He who has pity on the poor lends to the Lord, and He will pay back what he has given. —Proverbs 19:17

A father gave his little boy fifty cents and told him he could use it any way he wanted. Later, when the father asked what his son had decided to do with the money, the boy told him that he had lent it to someone.

"Who did you lend it to?" he asked.

The boy answered, "I gave it to a poor man on the street because he looked hungry."

"Oh, that was foolish. You'll never get it back," replied the father.

"But Daddy, the Bible says that people who give to the poor lend to the Lord."

The father was so pleased with his son's reply that he gave the boy another fifty cents. "See," said the son. "I told you I would get it back—only I didn't think it would be so soon!" (HB)

Cobwebs

How shall they believe in Him of whom they have not heard?
—*Romans 10:14*

A painter was commissioned to portray a run-down church. But instead of an old, tottering ruin, he painted a magnificent edifice of modern design. Through the windows could be seen an ornate collection box for the gifts of the fashionable worshipers. Above it hung a sign bearing the inscription "For Missions." Sadly, the box was covered in cobwebs. (DE)

God's Giving Standard

Though [Jesus] was rich, yet for your sakes He became poor, that you through His poverty might become rich.   —*2 Corinthians 8:9*

Stanford Kelly, a missionary to Haiti, provides a twenty-first century example of the kind of generosity Jesus demonstrated. After taking an offering in the little congregation where he served, Kelly found a gift of thirteen dollars. That was the equivalent of one month's wages in Haiti. The gift surprised him every bit as much as a $5,000 check would startle a pastor in a wealthier nation.

The extraordinary gift prompted Kelly to search out the giver, who was a farmer. When he questioned the man about his gift, the man was reluctant to answer. Kelly probed until he discovered that the man had sold his horse, even though the animal helped provide the man's livelihood.

"Why didn't you come to church to give the gift yourself?" Kelly asked.

The farmer replied, "Because I had no shirt to wear." (HR)

Cheerful Givers

God loves a cheerful giver.   —*2 Corinthians 9:7*

A pastor wanted to see if a farmer in his congregation was willing to support the Lord's work. So one day he challenged him with some direct questions. "If you had two farms," he asked, "would you be willing to give one to God?"

"Why, certainly!" replied the man. "I only wish I were in a position to do so."

The minister then asked, "If you had ten thousand dollars, would you give five thousand dollars to the Lord?"

Without hesitation the man responded, "How I'd love to have that kind of money! I'd enjoy giving generously like that."

Then the preacher asked this pointed question: "If you had two pigs, would you give one to the church?"

The farmer hesitated for a moment and then blurted out, "That's not fair. You know I've got two pigs!" (RD)

Greatest Is He Who Serves

Whoever desires to be first among you, let him be your slave.
—*Matthew 20:27*

A noncommissioned officer was directing the repairs of a military building during the American Revolution. He was barking orders to the soldiers under his command, trying to get them to raise a heavy wooden beam.

As the soldiers struggled in vain to lift the beam into place, a man who was passing by stopped to ask the one in charge why he wasn't helping the men. With all the pomp of an emperor, the soldier responded, "Sir, I am a corporal!"

"You are, are you?" replied the passerby. "I was not aware of that." Then, taking off his hat and bowing, he said, "I ask your pardon, Corporal." Then the stranger walked over and strained with the soldiers to lift the heavy beam.

After the job was finished, the man turned and said, "Mr. Corporal, when you have another such job and have not enough men, send for your Commander in Chief and I will come and help you a second time."

The corporal was thunderstruck. The person speaking to him was General Washington!

God measures greatness by service. (HB)

GOD

Foot-Washing God

[Jesus] poured water into a basin and began to wash the disciples'
feet.   *—John 13:5*

Questions about God's existence often troubled H. A. Hodges,
a brilliant young professor of philosophy at Oxford University.
One day as he strolled down the street, he passed by an art store.
His attention was captured by a picture in the window—a painting of Jesus kneeling to wash His disciples' feet.

Hodges knew the story recorded in John 13—God incar-
nate washing human feet. But suddenly the true meaning of
that scene gripped the heart of this young philosopher. God—
God!—humbling himself to do that lowliest of tasks! He
thought, *If God is like that, then that God shall be my God!*

Seeing that painting was one of the circumstances that
caused Hodges to surrender his life to the true God—the foot-
washing God. (VG)

Communion on the Moon

If I ascend into heaven, You are there.   *—Psalm 139:8*

Apollo 11 landed on the surface of the moon on Sunday, July 20,
1969. Most of us are familiar with Armstrong's historic state-
ment as he stepped onto the moon's surface: "That's one small
step for a man; one giant leap for mankind." But few know about
the first meal eaten there.

Buzz Aldrin had brought aboard the spacecraft a tiny communion kit provided by his church. After the landing, he sent

a radio broadcast to earth asking listeners to contemplate the events of that day and to give thanks.

Then, in radio blackout for privacy, Aldrin poured wine into a silver chalice. He read, "I am the vine, you are the branches. He who abides in Me, and I in him, bears much fruit" (John 15:5). Silently, he gave thanks and partook of the bread and cup. (DF)

Do We Know God?

This is eternal life, that they may know You, the only true God, and Jesus Christ whom You have sent. —John 17:3

American writer Mark Twain was known for his wit and charm. On a trip to Europe he was invited to dinner with a head of state. When his daughter learned of the invitation, she said, "Daddy, you know every big person there is to know except God." Sadly, that was true, because Mark Twain was an unbelieving skeptic. (VG)

What We Cannot Lose

Even to your old age, I am He,
And even to gray hairs I will carry you!
I have made, and I will bear;
Even I will carry, and will deliver you.
—Isaiah 46:4

Years ago I heard about an elderly gentleman who was suffering from the first stages of dementia. He lamented the fact that he often forgot about God. "Don't you worry," said a good friend. "He will never forget you." (DR)

GOD'S GUIDANCE

THE BEAUTIFUL THING ABOUT THIS ADVENTURE CALLED
FAITH IS THAT WE CAN COUNT ON HIM NEVER TO
LEAD US ASTRAY. —CHARLES SWINDOLL

No Error!

A man's heart plans his way, but the Lord directs his steps.
—Proverbs 16:9

The Dayspring Chorale, a traveling high school singing group, arrived at a nursing home for a Thursday concert. However, the folks at the home were expecting them on Friday. But they said if the group could get set up fast, they could sing for twenty minutes. Then they'd have to stop because there was going to be a memorial service for one of the residents.

The chorale hurriedly got ready and sang, and as they did, the son of the man who had died heard them. When they were done, he asked if they could sing at his dad's service. They gladly agreed and ministered hope and truth to all who attended.

God used these young people in a special way—all because of a secretarial error. But if we're doing God's will, we'll be in the right place. Then, wherever we are, we can point people to Him. (DB)

Timely Visit

After they had come to Mysia, they tried to go into Bithynia, but the Spirit did not permit them. *—Acts 16:7*

ODB writer Marvin Williams tells this story: On Friday, my day of rest as a pastor, the Holy Spirit prompted me to call a young single mother in our faith community to see if her car had been repaired. I had some reservations about making the call, but I obeyed.

Little did I know that my obedience would help save her life. She said later: "Friday at work I was planning on taking my life; but in a time of need, I believe God was there for me. He had Pastor Williams call me, and just by listening to his voice, I knew that God loved me." (MW)

Reformation

The king stood by a pillar and made a covenant before the Lord...
And all the people took a stand for the covenant. —2 Kings 23:3

In May of 2001, English evangelist J. John spoke in Liverpool, England, on the eighth commandment: "You shall not steal." The results of his preaching were dramatic.

People's hearts were changed. It was reported that large amounts of stolen goods were returned, including hotel towels, hospital crutches, library books, cash, and more. One man, who is now in the ministry, even returned towels he had taken from the Wimbledon tennis championships years earlier when he worked there.

When people read, hear, and obey God's Word, it should cause them to take immediate action to bring their lives into harmony with God's desires. (MW)

Another Walk with Whitaker

He leads me. —Psalm 23:2

ODB writer Dave Egner and his dog Whitaker like to take early-morning walks through the woods. "He runs ahead while I amble along, meditating or praying," says Dave. "I know where we're going; he's not sure. I stay on the trail and he trots ahead— sniffing, investigating, and taking occasional forays into the forest to chase real or imagined chipmunks.

"Though Whit is ahead, I'm leading. Every so often he checks to see where I am. If I've turned back toward home or gone on to another trail, I hear his pounding feet and panting breath as he races to catch up with me. If I hide behind some brush, he runs to the last place he saw me and tracks me down. Then we walk the trail together again."

It's like that with God's leading. (DE)

A Surprise Answer

Whatever we ask we receive from Him, because we keep His commandments and do those things that are pleasing in His sight.
—1 John 3:22

When Josh McDowell's mother died, he was not sure of her salvation. He became depressed. Was she a Christian or not? "Lord," he prayed, "somehow give me the answer so I can get back to normal. I've just got to know." It seemed like an impossible request.

Two days later, Josh drove out to the ocean and walked to the end of a pier to be alone. There sat an elderly woman in a lawn chair, fishing. "Where's your home originally?" she asked.

"Michigan. Union City," Josh replied. "Nobody's heard of it. I tell people it's a suburb of—"

"Battle Creek," interrupted the woman. "I had a cousin from there. Did you know the McDowell family?"

Stunned, Josh responded, "Yes, I'm Josh McDowell."

"I can't believe it," said the woman. "I'm a cousin to your mother."

"Do you remember anything at all about my mother's spiritual life?" asked Josh.

"Why sure. Your mom and I were just girls—teenagers—when a tent revival came to town. We both went forward to accept Christ."

"Praise God!" shouted Josh, startling the surrounding fishermen.

God delights to give us what we ask when it is in His will. (DD)

Mysterious Ways

[God] works all things according to the counsel of His will.

—Ephesians 1:11

The twists and turns in the life of Jacob DeShazer sound like the plot of an intriguing war novel. But taken together, they show us the mysterious ways in which God moves.

DeShazer served the U.S. Army Air Corps in World War II as a bombardier in the squadron of General Doolittle. While participating in Doolittle's raid on Japan in 1942, DeShazer and his crew ran out of fuel and bailed out over China, where DeShazer was captured and taken to a Japanese prison camp. During his imprisonment, he trusted Jesus as his Savior, and after his release, he became a missionary to Japan.

One day DeShazer handed a tract with his story in it to a man named Mitsuo Fuchida. He didn't know that Mitsuo was on his way to a trial for his wartime role as the commander of Japanese forces that attacked Pearl Harbor. Fuchida read the pamphlet and got a Bible. He soon became a Christian and an evangelist to his people. Eventually, DeShazer and Fuchida met again and became friends. (DB)

Life's Surprises

The Lord does not see as man sees; for man looks at the outward appearance, but the Lord looks at the heart.   *—1 Samuel 16:7*

No one watching *Britain's Got Talent* (a popular televised talent show) expected much when mobile phone salesman Paul Potts took the stage. The judges looked skeptically at one another when the nervous, unassuming, ordinary-looking chap announced he would sing opera—until Potts opened his mouth.

He began to sing Puccini's "Nessun Dorma"—and it was magical! The crowd roared and stood in amazement while the judges sat stunned in tearful silence. It was one of the greatest surprises any such television program has ever had, in large part because it came wrapped in such an ordinary package.

In the Old Testament, the rescuer of Israel arrived at the battlefield in a most unlikely form—a young shepherd boy (1 Samuel 17). (BC)

GOD'S LOVE

GOD LOVES EACH OF US AS IF THERE WERE ONLY ONE OF US. —ST. AUGUSTINE

"Daddy, I Found You!"

We love Him because He first loved us. —1 John 4:19

In his book *Jesus Among Other Gods,* Ravi Zacharias tells a story about a girl who became hopelessly lost in a dark and dense forest. She called and screamed, but to no avail. Her alarmed parents and a group of volunteers searched frantically for her. When darkness fell, they had to give up for the night.

Early the next morning the girl's father reentered the forest to search for her and spied her fast asleep on a rock. He called her name and ran toward her. Startled awake, she threw her arms out to him. As he picked her up and hugged her, she repeated over and over, "Daddy, I found you!" (HVL)

He Knows His Own

The Lord knows those who are His. —2 Timothy 2:19

Arctic sea birds called guillemots live on rocky coastal cliffs, where thousands of them come together in small areas. Because of the crowded conditions, the females lay their eggs side by side in a long row. It's incredible, but the mother birds can identify the eggs that belong to them. Studies show that even when an egg is moved some distance away, the mother finds it and carries it back to its original location.

As amazing as this is, our heavenly Father is far more intimately acquainted with each of His children. (MD)

——————— Doubting His Goodness ———————

He who did not spare His own Son, but delivered Him up for us all, how shall He not with Him also freely give us all things?
—Romans 8:32

A man in Dundee, Scotland, who had fallen and broken his back, was confined to his bed for forty years. He never had a day without pain, but God gave him grace and strength. His cheery disposition and great love for the Lord inspired all who visited him.

One day a friend asked, "Doesn't the devil ever tempt you to doubt God?"

"Oh yes, he tries—especially when I have to lie here and see my old schoolmates driving by, having a good time with their families. At times it's as if Satan whispers, 'If the Lord is so good, why does He keep you here? Why did He allow you to break your back?'"

When the friend asked how he handled such attacks, the man replied, "I point him to Calvary and to the wounds of my Savior and say, 'Doesn't He love me!' The devil can't answer that, so he flees every time."

That man's faith in God's love laid to rest any doubts about God's goodness. (HB)

GOD'S PRESENCE

I WOULD RATHER WALK WITH GOD IN
THE DARK THAN GO ALONE IN THE LIGHT.
—MARY GARDINER BRAINARD

He's Always Watching

The eye of the Lord is on those who fear Him, on those who hope in His mercy. —Psalm 33:18

A high school girl had broken up with her boyfriend, and now he was harassing her. He followed her, stared at her, and intimidated her in subtle ways. She avoided him as much as she could, but one place she could not escape his gaze was at football games, because she was a cheerleader. During one game, he stood at field level right in front of the cheerleading squad and stared at her as she did her routines. Her mom and stepdad, sitting in the stands, saw him there and realized that she was getting more and more afraid.

At a break, she ran into the stands, her eyes filled with panic. "Do you see him over there?" she blurted out.

"Yes, I do," her stepdad said. "I'm watching, and I will not take my eyes off you."

Relieved that he saw what was going on, understood how she was feeling, and was keeping his eyes on the situation, the girl calmed down and went back to her cheerleading.

One of the wonderful joys of being a believer in Jesus is knowing that our Father in heaven is always watching over us. (DE)

Rock Solid

The eyes of the Lord are on the righteous, and His ears are open to their cry.   —Psalm 34:15

It was a sad day in May 2003 when "The Old Man of the Mountain" broke apart and slid down the mountainside. This forty-foot profile of an old man's face, carved by nature in the White Mountains of New Hampshire, had long been an attraction for tourists, a solid presence for residents, and the official state emblem. Nathaniel Hawthorne wrote about it in his short story "The Great Stone Face."

Some nearby residents were devastated when The Old Man fell. One woman said, "I grew up thinking that someone was watching over me. I feel a little less watched-over now."

God is the Rock whose presence we can *always* depend on. He continually watches over us. (AC)

Invisible Companions

You have come to . . . an innumerable company of angels, to the general assembly.   —Hebrews 12:22–23

"One Sunday morning while traveling in West Virginia," *ODB* author Herb Vander Lugt recalled, "we visited a small church in a tiny village. Only fifteen people were present, yet they radiated joy as they sang. And the pastor preached from the Bible with enthusiasm. But I couldn't shake a feeling of sympathy for him and his people. With little chance for growth, it looked like a discouraging ministry."

Some time later, the testimony of a young seminarian showed Herb how wrong he was. Assigned to minister in a small village chapel, the young man was dismayed when only two people stayed for the communion service. As he read from the liturgy, he came to the words: "Therefore, with angels and archangels and all the company of heaven, we worship and adore Thy glorious name." That sentence changed everything for him. In his heart he said, "God forgive me. I did not know I was in that great company." (HVL)

I Will Come Back for You

I will not leave you orphans; I will come to you. —John 14:18

In 1914 Ernest Shackleton led an expedition to sail to Antarctica and then walk to the South Pole. The expedition went according to plan until, one hundred miles from their destination, the ship became trapped in sea ice, which eventually crushed and destroyed it. The men made their way in the lifeboats to a small island. Promising to come back for the rest of his crew, Shackleton and a small rescue party set out in one of the small lifeboats across eight hundred miles of perilous seas to South Georgia Island.

With only a sextant to guide them, they made it to the island. Shackleton then led his party over steep mountainous terrain to the whaling port on the other side. Once there, he acquired a ship to rescue his crew.

Their leader had kept his word and returned for them. Not one man was lost or left behind. (DF)

GRACE

GRACE IS THE FREE, UNDESERVED GOODNESS AND FAVOR OF GOD TO MANKIND. —MATTHEW HENRY

Rescued!

I will sing of the mercies of the Lord forever; with my mouth will I make known Your faithfulness to all generations. —Psalm 89:1

Cornerstone University president Joe Stowell says he'll never forget the first time he saw the Brooklyn Tabernacle Choir in concert. Nearly two hundred people who had been redeemed out of the bowels of Brooklyn—former crack addicts and prostitutes included—sang their hearts out to God. Their faces glistened with tears running down their cheeks as they sang about God's work of redemption and forgiveness in their lives.

As he watched them, Joe realized that since he was saved when he was six years old, he hadn't felt the same depth of gratefulness that these choir members displayed as they sang about the dramatic rescue God had provided for them.

"I was saved from things like biting my sister—not exactly a significant testimony," Stowell remarks.

Then the Spirit reminded him that if God had not rescued him when he was young, who knows where his life would be today? It became clear that he, too, was a great debtor to God's grace. It's not only what we are saved "out of" but what we have been saved "from" that makes our hearts worthy of a spot in the chorus of the redeemed. (JS)

Lessons of the Coke Bottle

Where sin abounded, grace abounded much more. —Romans 5:20

Pastor Louie was preaching on the pervasiveness of sin. "It's everywhere!" he stated emphatically. He described an incident when he was waiting for a traffic light: he saw a man in the car in front of him finish his Coke, open the door, set the glass bottle on the street, and drive away.

"That was wrong!" Pastor Louie said. "It was a selfish sin! He could have caused someone to have a flat tire or even an accident." We don't typically think of littering as sin, but it is clear evidence of our inherent selfishness.

Later, as the pastor was greeting people by the door, a Bible professor at a local Christian university said quietly as he walked by, "Sin puts the bottle on the street, but grace picks it up." (DE)

HEAVEN

No, it is not the jasper walls and the pearly gates
that are going to make heaven attractive. It is
the being with God. —Dwight L. Moody

Eager for Heaven

The street of the city was pure gold, like transparent glass.
—Revelation 21:21

"My neighbor Jasmine, age nine, was sitting on the front porch with me one summer evening," recalls *ODB* managing editor Anne Cetas. "Out of the blue she started talking about her bad choices and how she needed God's forgiveness. We talked and prayed together and she asked Jesus to be her Savior."

Questions about heaven started pouring out of Jasmine: "Are the streets really gold? Will my mom be there? What if she isn't? Will I have a bed, or will I sleep on a cloud? What will I eat?"

Anne assured her that heaven would be a perfect home and that she would be with Jesus, who would give her everything she needed. She replied with excitement, "Well, then, let's go right now!" (AC)

Loosening Our Grip

Since all these things will be dissolved, what manner of persons ought you to be?   *—2 Peter 3:11*

An American tourist traveled to Poland to visit with a respected religious teacher who was known for his wisdom. The visitor noticed that the man's room had nothing but a table, a chair, and some books. Puzzled by such austerity, he asked, "Where is your furniture?"

The teacher answered, "My furniture? Where is your furniture, my friend?"

The American protested, "Furniture? But I am only a tourist passing through."

"So am I," said the man.

And so are all of us. Because we're just passing through this world, we need to learn to loosen our grip on our earthly possessions. (VG)

The Upside of Dying

Father, I desire that they also whom You gave Me may be with Me where I am, that they may behold My glory.   — John 17:24

A Sunday school teacher asked some five-year-olds a series of questions to help them realize that trusting in Jesus is the only way to get to heaven. He asked, "If I sell everything I have and give the money to the church, would that get me into heaven?"

"No," they answered.

"How about if I keep everything clean in and around the church?"

Another no.

"If I love my family, am kind to animals, and give candy to every child I meet, will that get me to heaven?"

Another unanimous no!

Then he asked, "What will get me into heaven?"

A little boy shouted, "You have to be dead!"

This was hardly the answer the teacher expected, but the youngster was right. The Bible tells us that someday we all must leave our flesh-and-blood bodies (1 Corinthians 15:50–53). (HVL)

The Journey Home

[Abraham] waited for the city . . . whose builder and maker is God.
—Hebrews 11:10

Bill Bright, the founder of Campus Crusade for Christ, was diagnosed years ago with the terminal disease pulmonary fibrosis.

Eventually he required prolonged bed rest. Bright used this time of quiet reflection to write a book called *The Journey Home*.

In his book, Bright quoted Charles Haddon Spurgeon, who said, "May we live here like strangers and make the world not a house, but an inn, in which we sup and lodge, expecting to be on our journey tomorrow."

Struck by Spurgeon's perspective concerning his own terminal prognosis, Bright commented, "Knowing that heaven is our real home makes it easier to pass through the tough times here on earth. I have taken comfort often in the knowledge that the perils of a journey on earth will be nothing compared to the glories of heaven." (DF)

HELPING OTHERS

GOOD EXERCISE FOR THE HEART: BENDING DOWN AND
HELPING ANOTHER UP. —AUTHOR UNKNOWN

Widows' Pain

You shall not afflict any widow or fatherless child. If you afflict them in any way, and they cry at all to Me, I will surely hear their cry. —Exodus 22:22–23

CNN reported that there are approximately forty million widows in India. Fifteen thousand of them live on the streets of the northern city of Vrindavan. Unfortunately, many of their families do not hear their cries.

A seventy-year-old widow says, "My son tells me: 'You have grown old. Now who is going to feed you? Go away.' "

She cries, "What do I do? My pain has no limit."

When God gave His people instructions in the desert, He told them they had a responsibility to care for widows and fatherless children in the land. They were to leave some of the harvest in the field for them, and every third year they took up a special tithe for the needy. God expected His people to hear the cries of the powerless, defend their rights, and care for them.

Let us imitate our Father by hearing the cries of the needy in our world. (MW)

Giving Others a Push

[He] encouraged them all that with purpose of heart they should continue with the Lord. —Acts 11:23

When Jean was a teenager, she often walked through a park where she saw mothers sitting on benches and talking. Their toddlers sat on the swings, wanting someone to push them.

"I gave them a push," says Jean. "And you know what happens when you push a kid on a swing? Pretty soon he's pumping, doing it himself. That's what my role in life is—I'm there to give others a push." (AC)

Food Flight

Do not forget to entertain strangers, for by so doing some have unwittingly entertained angels. —Hebrews 13:2

While Bill Crowder was taking a flight to Surabaya, Indonesia, for a Bible conference, the flight attendants brought meal service. Bill had just eaten in the Singapore airport, so he declined, asking only for a soft drink. The Indonesian man next to him, a stranger, was visibly concerned.

The man asked if Bill felt okay, and Crowder assured him he was fine. The man then asked Bill if perhaps the meal didn't appeal to him. Bill responded that he just wasn't hungry. The man then surprised Bill by offering his own meal to him, thinking that if he tried it he might actually enjoy it.

"He did it in such a gentle and genuine way," says Bill, "that it was obviously an expression of his concern for my welfare." (BC)

A Good Sign

Some indeed preach Christ even from envy and strife, and some also from goodwill. —Philippians 1:15

A pastor told about a sign he had seen in front of a neighborhood church. Instead of just advertising the congregation's own time of worship, the sign also listed the schedule for two other churches that met at different times in the same small town. Interestingly, the pastor telling about the sign didn't think this was impractical or foolish. Instead, he imagined what it must do for a church to put such unselfishness at the heart of everything it did! (MD)

Unexpected Help

The woman took the two men and hid them. —Joshua 2:4

In 1803, Thomas Jefferson commissioned Lewis and Clark to lead an expedition across an unexplored America to the Pacific coast. The expedition was called "Corps of Discovery"—and it lived up to its name. The explorers cataloged three hundred new species, identified nearly fifty Indian tribes, and traversed terrain that had never been seen by Europeans.

They were joined along the way by a French fur trader and his wife Sacajawea. Lewis and Clark soon found her to be invaluable as an interpreter and guide.

During the trip, Sacajawea was reunited with her family. Her older brother had become the tribe's chief, and he helped them acquire horses and a map of the uncharted West. Without Sacajawea's and her brother's unexpected help, the expedition may not have succeeded. (DF)

Heart for Others

Greater love has no one than this, than to lay down one's life for his friends.   *—John 15:13*

As the young people in a high school chorale set up for a concert in the town square in Montego Bay, Jamaica, the worst problem they anticipated was sunburn.

The chorale was in Jamaica to encourage Christians and to spread the gospel through music. They had been looking forward to this outreach event.

Midway through the concert, a woman who didn't like the message of the music began shouting angrily at the chorale. Apparently, the God-honoring songs were more than she could stand. After several tense minutes, a bystander tried to quiet her. A fight broke out, and the adult chaperones began to fear for the safety of the young people. Finally, the woman ran away, and the chorale finished the concert.

Later, one of the adults in charge of the kids said to one of the girls, "Well, we won't do that again," indicating that the top priority was to protect her and her friends.

The girl responded, "If one person came to know Jesus, it was worthwhile, even if we were in danger." (DB)

A Timely Word

A man has joy by the answer of his mouth, and a word spoken in due season, how good it is!   *—Proverbs 15:23*

In Liverpool, England, on the eve of the 2006 British Open Championship, professional golfer Graeme McDowell was in trouble. He was concerned because he was going into the tournament clueless about what was causing his struggles on the course.

While he was out for the evening, McDowell got a surprise. A stranger, who was an avid golf fan, recognized him and commented that he had noticed a flaw in his swing. The next day, Graeme tested the man's advice on the driving range, and to his great shock he discovered that the fan was correct. Graeme implemented the suggestion and finished the first day of the British Open in first place! All because a stranger took time to speak a word of help. (BC)

HISTORY

IF YOU WANT TO UNDERSTAND TODAY, YOU HAVE TO SEARCH YESTERDAY. —PEARL S. BUCK

Taps

Your sun shall no longer go down... for the Lord will be your ever-lasting light, and the days of your mourning shall be ended.
—Isaiah 60:20

In 1862, during the U.S. Civil War, General Daniel Butterfield wanted a new melody for "lights out." And so, without any musical training, he composed one in his head.

Years later, the general wrote, "I called in someone who could write music, and practiced a change in the call of 'Taps' until I had it suit my ear, and then... got it to my taste without being able to write music or knowing the technical name of any note, but, simply by ear, arranged it." General Butterfield gave the music to the brigade bugler, and the rest is history.

For those who follow Jesus, the strains of "Taps" are not a funeral dirge but a song of hope. "The days of your mourning shall be ended." All is well. God is nigh. (TG)

Abe's Best

When they speak against you as evildoers, they may, by your good works which they observe, glorify God.   —1 Peter 2:12

Abraham Lincoln knew what it meant to face criticism. He is quoted as saying, "If I were to try to read, much less answer, all the attacks made on me, this shop might as well be closed for any other business. I do the very best I know how—the very best I can; and I mean to keep doing so until the end. If the end brings me out all right, what's said against me won't amount to anything. If the end brings me out wrong, ten angels swearing I was right would make no difference." (BC)

Late News

Having been set free from sin, you became slaves of righteousness.
—Romans 6:18

On June 19, 1865, more than two years after President Lincoln had signed the Emancipation Proclamation, General Gordon Granger rode into Galveston, Texas, and read General Order Number 3: "The people of Texas are informed that in accordance with a Proclamation from the Executive of the United States, all slaves are free."

For the first time, slaves in Texas learned that they were already free. Some were shocked; many others celebrated. June 19 soon became known as "Juneteenth." (MW)

Bad Hunk of Stone

[You] have put on the new man who is renewed in knowledge according to the image of Him who created him.   —Colossians 3:10

For almost one hundred years a huge piece of flawed Carrara marble lay in the courtyard of a cathedral in Florence, Italy. Then, in 1501, a young sculptor was asked to do something with it. He measured the block and noted its imperfections. In his mind, he envisioned a young shepherd boy.

For three years he chiseled and shaped the marble skillfully. Finally, when the eighteen-foot towering figure of David was unveiled, a student exclaimed to Michelangelo, "Master, it lacks only one thing—speech!" (AL)

Locked Up, Not Out

He shall make restitution for his trespass in full. —*Numbers 5:7*

During the compilation of the *Oxford English Dictionary,* managing editor James Murray received thousands of definitions from Dr. William Chester Minor. They were always sent in by mail and never brought in personally. Murray was curious about this brilliant man, so he went to visit him. He was shocked to find that Minor was incarcerated in an asylum for the criminally insane.

Years earlier, while in a delusional state, Minor had shot an innocent man whom he thought had been tormenting him. Later, he was filled with remorse and began sending money to support the widow and her family. Minor was imprisoned for the rest of his life, but he found practical ways of easing the pain of his victims and contributing to society through his work on the dictionary. (DF)

HUMOR

HE WHO LAUGHS, LASTS. —MARY PETTIBONE POOLE

Good and Bad Laughter

To everything there is a season, a time for every purpose under heaven... A time to laugh. —*Ecclesiastes 3:1, 4*

Joe E. Brown was a top-notch movie and Broadway comedian of the World War II era. When entertaining American troops in the South Pacific, he was asked by a soldier to tell some "dirty jokes." He responded, "Son, a comedian like me lives for applause and laughter. But if telling a dirty story is the price I must pay for your laughter, then I'm not interested. I've never done an act that I couldn't perform before my mother, and I never will." The soldiers rocked the jungle with their cheers.

Lord, give us a merry heart. And help us be discerning so that we will laugh for the right reasons and about the right things. (HVL)

What God Owes Us

Walk worthy of the Lord, fully pleasing Him. —Colossians 1:10

A story is told about a vendor who sold bagels for fifty cents each at a streetcorner food stand. A jogger ran past and threw a couple of quarters into the bucket but didn't take a bagel. He did the same thing every day for months.

One day as the jogger was passing by, the vendor stopped him. The jogger asked, "You probably want to know why I always put money in but never take a bagel, don't you?"

"No," said the vendor. "I just wanted to tell you that the bagels have gone up to sixty cents." (CHK)

On Purpose

All things work together for good... to those who are the called according to His purpose. —Romans 8:28

When a cowboy applied for an insurance policy, the agent asked, "Have you ever had any accidents?"

After a moment's reflection, the applicant responded, "Nope, but a bronc did kick in two of my ribs last summer, and a couple of years ago a rattlesnake bit me on the ankle."

"Wouldn't you call those accidents?" replied the puzzled agent.

"Naw," the cowboy said, "they did it on purpose!" (RD)

No Sale

Peter said to him, "Your money perish with you, because you thought that the gift of God could be purchased with money!" —Acts 8:20

Police officers in St. Louis have had at least one easy arrest. It occurred at the back door of the police station when a drunk driver pulled his car right up to the booking window, thinking he was at Burger King. After attempting to place his order at what he thought was a drive-up window, the surprised driver was arrested by the booking officer and charged with drunk driving. (MD)

A Matter of Taste

Let us cleanse ourselves from all filthiness of the flesh and spirit.
—2 Corinthians 7:1

Two cockroaches decided to visit their favorite restaurant. While the larger of the two was enjoying his meal, the smaller one said, "You wouldn't believe the house I just left. It was spotless. The lady had to be a cleanaholic. Everything was immaculate—the sink, the counter, the floors. You couldn't find a crumb anywhere."

The other cockroach stopped his munching, looked with some annoyance at his companion, and said, "Do you have to talk like that while I'm eating?" (MD)

Keeping the Elephants Away

Be anxious for nothing, but in everything by prayer... let your requests be made known to God. —Philippians 4:6

A man was sitting on a park bench shredding old newspapers and spreading them around. "What are you doing?" asked a bystander.

"I'm spreading this paper around to keep the elephants away."

The visitor looked around the well-kept city park. "I don't see any elephants," he said.

The man smiled. "Works pretty good, doesn't it," he replied. (DD)

Hiding from God

The Lord God said to the woman, "What is this you have done?"
—Genesis 3:13

Two brothers were extremely mischievous, and their parents were at their wits' end. So they asked their pastor to talk with the boys.

The pastor sat the younger one down first. He wanted the boy to think about God, so he started the conversation by asking, "Where is God?" The boy didn't respond, so he repeated the question in a stern tone. Again he gave no answer. Frustrated, the pastor shook his finger in the boy's face and shouted, "Where is God?!"

The boy bolted from the room, ran home, and hid in his closet. His brother followed him and asked, "What happened?"

The younger boy replied, "We're in big trouble now. God is missing, and they think we did it!" (AC)

Submissive Leadership

… submitting to one another in the fear of God.   —Ephesians 5:21

A mild-mannered man was reading a book on being self-assertive and decided to start at home. So he stormed into his house, pointed a finger in his wife's face, and said, "From now on I'm boss around here and my word is law! I want you to prepare me a gourmet meal and draw my bath. Then, when I've eaten and finished my bath, guess who's going to dress me and comb my hair."

"The mortician," replied his wife. (AC)

Who Calls the Game?

Shall the one who contends with the Almighty correct Him?

—Job 40:2

During an afternoon baseball game when American League umpire Bill Guthrie was working behind home plate, the catcher for the visiting team repeatedly protested his calls.

According to a story in the *St. Louis Post Dispatch,* Guthrie endured this for three innings. But in the fourth inning, when the catcher started to complain again, Guthrie stopped him. "Son," he said gently, "you've been a big help to me calling balls and strikes, and I appreciate it. But I think I've got the hang of it now. So I'm going to ask you to go to the clubhouse and show them how to take a shower." (MD)

Humbled

God led you all the way these forty years ... to humble you and test you, to know what was in your heart. *—Deuteronomy 8:2*

A Texas farmer was talking with a farmer from Oklahoma. "How big is your farm?" asked the Texan.

"Oh, it's big," replied the Sooner. "Better than a thousand acres."

Not to be outdone, the Texan replied, "Let me tell you. I can get into my pickup at sunup, head west, and by sundown I'm still on my land."

The Oklahoman thought for a moment and smiled. "You know," he said, "I had a pickup like that once!" (DD)

Excuses, Excuses, Excuses

Then the man said, "The woman whom You gave to be with me, she gave me of the tree, and I ate." *—Genesis 3:12*

The manager of a minor league baseball team was tired of watching his center fielder play poorly, according to a story by Don McCullough in *Discipleship Journal.* So he grabbed a glove and headed for the outfield to show the player how it should be done.

The first ball hit toward him took a bad hop and hit the manager in the mouth. Next came a high fly ball that he lost in the sun—only to find it when it smacked him on his forehead. Later a hard line drive missed his glove and hit him in the face. That was enough. Furious, the manager grabbed the center fielder by the uniform and shouted, "You idiot! You've got center field so messed up, even I can't do a thing with it!" (DB)

INTEGRITY

IT TAKES LESS TIME TO DO A THING RIGHT, THAN IT
DOES TO EXPLAIN WHY YOU DID IT WRONG.
—HENRY WADSWORTH LONGFELLOW

A Wonderful Pair

What is desired in a man is kindness, and a poor man is better than a liar.   —*Proverbs 19:22*

An honest and kind man drove the streets of San Francisco for more than an hour to find the woman who had left her purse with $1,792 in cash on the back seat of his cab. When some of his fellow drivers ridiculed him for not pocketing the money, he responded, "I am a card-carrying member of the Christian faith, and what good is it to go to church if you don't practice what you preach?" (HVL)

Integrity 101

I will behave wisely in a perfect way . . . I will walk within my house with a perfect heart.   —*Psalm 101:2*

Officials in Philadelphia were astonished to receive a letter and payment from a motorist who had been given a speeding ticket in 1954. John Gedge, an English tourist, had been visiting the City of Brotherly Love when he was cited for speeding. The penalty was $15, but Gedge forgot about the ticket for almost fifty-two years until he discovered it in an old coat.

"I thought, I've got to pay it," said Gedge, eighty-four, who now lives in a nursing home in East Sussex. "Englishmen pay their debts. My conscience is clear." (MW)

Which Tire Was It?

You have not lied to men but to God. —Acts 5:4

One sunny day, four high school boys couldn't resist the temptation to skip classes. The next morning they explained to their teacher that they had missed her class because their car had a flat tire. To their relief, she smiled and said, "Well, you missed a quiz yesterday." But then she added, "Take your seats and get out a pencil and paper. The first question is: Which tire was flat?" (DD)

Rock-Solid Integrity

Lord, who may abide in Your tabernacle? Who may dwell in Your holy hill? He who walks uprightly, and works righteousness, and speaks the truth in his heart. —Psalm 15:1–2

A young man named Mike meets the psalmist's definition of integrity. He's a college graduate with a degree in construction management and is trying to get started with a good company. He was delighted, therefore, when a local firm hired him. He went to work filled with enthusiasm and a desire to please his new employers. It wasn't long, however, before his supervisor was asking him to make misleading statements to customers about materials and costs. After a brief inner struggle, he shared his dilemma with his wife, Alice. They prayed together and asked the Lord what he should do.

The next day Mike told his boss he would not lie to customers and suppliers. That Friday he was laid off. He knew why. He also knew he would never be called back. (DE)

The Art of Common People

I have not come to call the righteous, but sinners, to repentance.
—Luke 5:32

The sixteenth-century Italian painter Caravaggio received scathing criticism in his day for depicting people of the Bible as commoners. His critics reflected the viewpoint of the time— that only members of royalty and the aristocracy were appropriate subjects for the "immortality" of art. His commissioned canvas of *St. Matthew and the Angel* so offended church leaders that it had to be redone. They could not accept seeing Matthew with the physical features and garb of an everyday laborer.

According to one biographer, what the church fathers did not understand was that "Caravaggio, in elevating this humble figure, was copying Christ, who had Himself raised Matthew from the street."

Caravaggio was right about the people of the Bible. Jesus himself grew up in the home of a laborer. When His time came to go public, He was announced by a weatherworn man of the wilderness known as John the Baptizer. His disciples were fishermen and common people.

Jesus lived, loved, and died for wealthy people too. But by befriending fishermen, lepers, widows, and even despised tax collectors, the teacher from Nazareth showed that no one is too poor, too sinful, or too insignificant to be His friend. (MD)

"Was that Jesus?"

Imitate me, just as I also imitate Christ.   —1 Corinthians 11:1

The story is told of a Christian who was home on furlough from serving in the armed forces. He was rushing to catch his train when he ran into a fruit stand on the station platform, knocking most of the piled-up apples to the ground.

The young boy who operated the stand tried to pick up his scattered fruit but was having difficulty. The apologetic serviceman put down his luggage and started collecting the apples. He polished each one with his handkerchief and put it back on the counter.

So impressed was the boy that he asked gratefully, "Soldier, are you Jesus?"

With a smile the soldier replied, "No, but I'm trying to be like Him." (VG)

Haley's Experiment

[I pray] that they all may be one, as You, Father, are in Me, and I in You.
—John 17:21

In doing research for his epic story *Roots,* Alex Haley embarked on the freighter *African Star,* sailing from Monrovia, Liberia, to Jacksonville, Florida. He did so to better understand the travails of his ancestors, who were brought in chains to America.

Haley descended into the ship's hold, stripped himself of protective clothing, and tried to sleep on some thick, rough-hewn bracing. After the third miserable night, he gave up and returned to his cabin. But he could now write with some small degree of empathy of the sufferings of his forebears. (VG)

Ultimate Help

These all died in faith, not having received the promises, but having seen them afar off were assured of them. —*Hebrews 11:13*

Missionary couple Ray and Sophie de le Haye served heroically in West Africa for more than forty years. As she grew older, Sophie suffered from the loss of all motor control of her body. The once-strong servant of Christ, who had carried on a ministry of unimaginable stress, was suddenly reduced to helplessness, unable to button her clothes or lift a cup of water to her lips. But she refused to become bitter or self-pitying. In her moments of utter weakness, she would quietly remind herself, "For this you have Jesus." (VG)

Deep Waters

No other foundation can anyone lay than that which is laid, which is Jesus Christ. —*1 Corinthians 3:11*

"While taking a break during a ministry trip, we were snorkeling in the Caribbean Sea," Dave Branon writes. "The boat that had taken us to the deep water for better sites had gone back to shore, and I began to feel panicky about being in the open water. Finding it hard to control my breathing, I asked my son-in-law Todd and a friend, Dave Velzen, for help. They held my arms while I searched for an outcropping of coral close enough to the surface for me to stand on. Once I had a place to stand, even though surrounded by deep waters, I was okay." (DB)

The Comeback King

A little while longer and the world will see Me no more, but you will see Me. Because I live, you will live also. —*John 14:19*

We admire anyone who makes a comeback after failure and defeat. In 2001, *Sports Illustrated* magazine featured an article on the greatest comebacks of all time. Surprisingly, they selected the resurrection of Jesus as number one. It was stated this way: "Jesus Christ, 33 AD. Defies critics and stuns the Romans with His resurrection." (VG)

Wounded for Me

He was wounded for our transgressions, He was bruised for our iniquities. —Isaiah 53:5

A man who was deeply troubled by his sins was having a vivid dream in which he saw Jesus being savagely whipped by a soldier. As the cruel scourge came down upon Christ's back, the onlooker shuddered, for the terrible cords left ugly, gaping wounds upon His bleeding, swollen body. When the one wielding the lash raised his arm to strike the Lord again, the man rushed forward to stop him. As he did, the soldier turned, and the dreamer was startled to see his own face! (HB)

"She Wouldn't Let Me"

Come to Me, all you who labor and are heavy laden, and I will give you rest. —Matthew 11:28

A woman was trapped on the top floor of a burning building. Flames and smoke blocked every way of escape. When firefighters arrived, one of the men scrambled up a ladder to the window where the woman was screaming for help, and with outstretched arms he offered to save her. But when she looked down and saw the great distance to the ground below, she panicked and drew back into the room.

The man attempting the rescue begged her to trust him for her safety, but his pleas were not heeded. In senseless fear she retreated beyond the fireman's reach. Finally, being forced to return to the ground, he said with tears in his eyes, "I did everything I could to save her, but she wouldn't let me!" (RD)

Name Above All Names

You shall call His name Jesus, for He will save His people from their sins. —Matthew 1:21

If you knew for certain that you were going to lose your voice and that you would never be able to speak again, what would you want your final words to be?

A man with throat cancer faced an operation that would save his life but not his voice. Just before surgery, he spent time with his wife telling her of his love. He did the same with his daughter.

Then he asked his doctor to let him know precisely when the anesthetic would make him unconscious. As the man was slipping off to sleep, he said distinctly, "Jesus! Jesus!" That was the last word he chose to utter in this life—"Jesus!" (VG)

Wonder

All those who heard it marveled at those things which were told them by the shepherds.   *—Luke 2:18*

In 1921, Elmer Kline, a bakery manager, was given the job of naming his company's new loaf of bread. As he struggled to come up with something "catchy," he found his answer in an unlikely place.

While visiting the grounds of the Indianapolis Motor Speedway, he stopped to watch the International Balloon Festival. Later he described the sight of the beautiful hot-air balloons launching into the Indiana sky as one of "awe and wonderment." The thought stuck, and he called the new product Wonder Bread. To this day, colorful balloons brighten the packaging for Wonder Bread.

Wonder, however, is a word that evokes something more significant than a loaf of bread or hot-air balloons. One dictionary defines *wonder* as "a cause of astonishment or admiration." It's a word that captures the experience of all the people who observed or heard about the events of the coming of Jesus into the world. (BC)

An Easy Yoke

Take My yoke upon you and learn from Me.   *—Matthew 11:29*

A Sunday school teacher read Matthew 11:30 to the children in her class, and then asked: "Jesus said, 'My yoke is easy.' Who can tell me what a yoke is?" A boy raised his hand and replied, "A yoke is something they put on the necks of animals so they can help each other."

Then the teacher asked, "What is the yoke Jesus puts on us?"

A quiet little girl raised her hand and said, "It is God putting His arm around us." (AC)

Get to Know Jesus

Grow in the grace and knowledge of our Lord and Savior Jesus Christ. —2 Peter 3:18

In his book *The Call*, Os Guinness tells a story about Arthur Burns, chairman of the U.S. Federal Reserve Board during the 1970s. Burns, who was Jewish, became part of a Bible study held at the White House at that time. One day, those in the group listened in surprise as Burns prayed, "O God, may the day come when all Jews will come to know Jesus." But an even bigger surprise came when he prayed for the time "when all Christians will come to know Jesus."

Burns hit on a profound truth we all need to wrestle with. Even if we claim the name of Jesus Christ, it may not be evident to others that we really know Him. (DB)

"Follow Me"

Jesus said to them, "Follow Me ..." They immediately left their nets and followed Him. —Mark 1:17–18

When the United States launched its space program in 1958, seven men were chosen to become the first astronauts. Imagine the excitement of Scott Carpenter, Gordon Cooper, John Glenn, Gus Grissom, Walter Schirra, Alan Shepard, and Deke Slayton. They were selected to go where no one had ever gone before.

Yet, as astronauts they knew they would face unforeseen dangers, challenges, and trials. The thrill of being chosen was tempered with the fear of the unknown future.

Imagine what another group of men must have felt when they were chosen for an important mission: the twelve apostles Jesus chose one day near the Sea of Galilee. (DB)

LIFE

TO LIVE IS SO STARTLING IT LEAVES LITTLE TIME FOR
ANYTHING ELSE. —EMILY DICKINSON

The Choice

I have set before you today life and good, death and evil.
—Deuteronomy 30:15

You've heard the infamous name of John Wilkes Booth. He assassinated President Abraham Lincoln in 1865. But have you heard about Edwin Booth, John's eldest brother? Edwin, a well-known actor, was waiting at a Jersey City train station when he saw someone slip and fall off the platform. Edwin quickly grabbed the man's collar and pulled him to safety, rescuing him from serious injury or death.

Who was the man he saved? Abraham Lincoln's son Robert, a soldier in the Civil War.

How ironic that the man who saved Lincoln's son had a brother who would soon kill the president. One saved a life; one took a life. One chose life; the other chose death. (AC)

Frozen Snowball

We are receiving a kingdom which cannot be shaken.
—Hebrews 12:28

Baseball pitcher Tug McGraw had a wonderful philosophy of pitching. He called it his "frozen snowball" theory.

"If I come in to pitch with the bases loaded," Tug explained, "and heavy hitter Willie Stargell is at bat, there's no reason I want to throw the ball. But eventually I have to pitch. So I remind myself that in a few billion years the earth will become a frozen snowball hurtling through space, and nobody's going to care what Willie Stargell did with the bases loaded!"

The Bible tells us the earth will someday "melt with fervent heat; both the earth and the works that are in it will be burned up" (2 Peter 3:10). Yet McGraw's point is valid: We need to keep life in perspective. Most of the things we worry about have no eternal significance. (HR)

LOVE

WHAT THE WORLD REALLY NEEDS IS MORE LOVE AND
LESS PAPERWORK. —PEARL BAILEY

Cab Cupid

Behold what manner of love the Father has bestowed on us, that we should be called children of God! —1 John 3:1

Some people looking for love have found help in an unusual place—a taxicab in New York City. Taxicab driver Ahmed Ibrahim loves to set up blind dates for his single passengers. His matchmaking services have been featured on the Fox News Channel, The *Wall Street Journal,* and NBC's *Today* show. He doesn't assist just anybody though; they have to be serious about looking to settle down with someone. Ahmed loves to help romance blossom, and he even hands out roses on Valentine's Day. (AC)

Arms of Love

Let us not love in word or in tongue, but in deed and in truth.

—1 John 3:18

Many college students go on summer missions trips. But rarely does one come back with a baby she has rescued. Mallery Thurlow, a student at Cornerstone University in Grand Rapids, went to Haiti to help distribute food. One day a mother showed up at the distribution center with a sick infant in her arms. The woman was out of options. The baby needed surgery, but no one would perform it. Without intervention, the baby would die. Mallery took baby Rose into her arms—and into her heart.

After returning to the U.S., Mallery searched for someone to operate on baby Rose. Most doctors held out little hope. Finally, Rose was granted a visa to leave Haiti, and Mallery went back to get her. Detroit Children's Hospital donated the $100,000 surgery, and it was successful. A little life was saved.

Like Mallery, we are called to love "in deed and in truth." Who needs you to be God's arms of love today? (DB)

A Mysterious Equation

God demonstrates His own love toward us, in that while we were still sinners, Christ died for us. *—Romans 5:8*

Professor John Nash of Princeton University is a math genius who has spent his life in the abstract world of numbers, equations—and delusions. Nash suffers from schizophrenia, a mental illness that can result in bizarre behavior and broken relationships. With medical help and the love of his wife, he learned to live with his illness and later won the Nobel Prize.

In the movie version of his life, Nash said: "I've always believed in numbers and the equations and logics that lead to reason... My quest has taken me through the physical, the metaphysical, the delusional, and back. And I've made the most important discovery of my life. It's only in the mysterious equations of love that any logical reasons can be framed." (DD)

How God Shows His Love

I have given you an example, that you should do as I have done to you.
                                                    —John 13:15

Martha, a twenty-six-year-old woman with ALS (amyotrophic lateral sclerosis), needed help. When a group of ladies from Evanston, Illinois, heard about her, they jumped into action. They began to give round-the-clock nursing care. They bathed her, fed her, prayed for her, and witnessed to her. Martha, who had not received Christ as her Savior and couldn't understand how a loving God could let her get ALS, saw His love in these women and eventually became a Christian.

Martha is with the Lord today because sixteen women, following Jesus' example, personified God's love. (HVL)

MONEY

A NICKEL AIN'T WORTH A DIME ANYMORE.
                —YOGI BERRA

Better Off

Incline your ear, and come to Me. Hear, and your soul shall live.
                                                    —Isaiah 55:3

A story is told of a wealthy man who felt that his son needed to learn gratefulness. So he sent him to stay with a poor farmer's family. After one month, the son returned. The father asked, "Now don't you appreciate what we have?"

The boy thought for a moment and said, "The family I stayed with is better off. With what they've planted, they enjoy meals together. And they always seem to have time for one another." (AL)

Garbage Mary

Lay aside all filthiness and overflow of wickedness, and receive with meekness the implanted word. —James 1:21

She dressed in rags, lived in a tenement house amid mounds of garbage, and spent much of her time rummaging through trash-cans. The local newspaper picked up her story after the woman who was known in her neighborhood as "Garbage Mary" had been admitted to a psychiatric hospital. Astonishingly, in her filthy apartment police found stock certificates and bankbooks indicating she was worth at least a million dollars. (MD)

Money Matters

No servant can serve two masters; for either he will hate the one and love the other, or else he will be loyal to the one and despise the other. —Luke 16:13

Godfrey Davis, who wrote a biography of the Duke of Wellington, said, "I found an old account ledger that showed how the Duke spent his money. It was a far better clue to what he thought was really important than the reading of his letters or speeches."

How we handle money reveals much about our priorities. (HR)

Graffiti

One's life does not consist in the abundance of the things he possesses. —Luke 12:15

Pastor and evangelist E. V. Hill went home to be with his Lord and Savior on February 25, 2003. He was much sought after as a conference speaker, and few gained the attention and respect of people from all levels of society as he did.

Many years ago, Pastor Hill was invited to speak in a suburban church of a large southern city in the United States. In the introduction to his message, Pastor Hill commented on the difference between the affluent suburb and the poor urban area where he ministered. "I know what's missing," he said. "You folks don't have any graffiti anywhere. I'd like to volunteer to provide some for you. I'll get a bucket of paint and walk through your neighborhood, writing this one word on your million-dollar homes and expensive European cars: *temporary*. That's it—temporary. None of it will last." (DE)

NEIGHBORS

A Good Neighbor

Which of these three do you think was neighbor to him who fell among the thieves?　　　　　　　　　　　　　*—Luke 10:36*

When Fred Rogers died on February 27, 2003, scores of newspapers carried the story as front-page news, and almost every headline included the word *neighbor*. As host of the long-running children's television show *Mr. Rogers' Neighborhood*, he was well known to millions of children and their parents as a kind, gentle, warm person who genuinely believed "each person is special, deep inside, just the way they are."

Mr. Rogers once told a journalist: "When we look at our neighbor with appreciative eyes... with gratitude for who that person truly is, then I feel we are arm in arm with Christ Jesus, the advocate of eternal good." (DM)

I'm in Debt

I am a debtor both to Greeks and to barbarians, both to wise and to unwise.　　　　　　　　　　　　　*—Romans 1:14*

A shopper underestimated the total cost of her groceries. When the cashier added up the items, the woman was four dollars short. Then something unusual happened. The man behind her in the checkout lane saw her digging through her purse and motioned to the clerk to put the amount on his bill. He modestly refused to give the woman his name.

A few days later, the local newspaper reported that a charity organization had received a four-dollar check with the following note: "This check is for the man who helped me out of a tight spot. I came up with the idea of giving it to you as a thank-you to him."

This incident illustrates a vital spiritual principle. We should feel an obligation to pass along to others the kindnesses shown to us. (MD)

Megan's Heart

Be doers of the word, and not hearers only. —James 1:22

When Megan was in third grade, she kept coming home from school without her winter gloves. It drove her mom crazy because she had to keep buying new ones, which the family couldn't afford. One day Mom got angry and said, "Megan, you've got to be more responsible. This can't go on!"

Megan began to cry. Through her tears she told her mom that as long as she kept getting new gloves, she could give hers away to kids who didn't have any.

Now at age eighteen, Megan's hobbies include volunteering in the community and mentoring inner-city kids. Referring to her desire to help people, she said that it "felt like that was the kind of thing I was supposed to be doing." (AC)

Neighborly Love

Love your neighbor as yourself. —Matthew 22:39

The Carnegie Foundation discovered that to be successful on the job, relational skills are far more important than knowledge. Its research found that only 15 percent of a person's success is determined by job knowledge and technical skills. Eighty-five percent is determined by an individual's attitude and ability to relate to other people. (VG)

Passed By

Whatever you want men to do to you, do also to them, for this is the Law and the Prophets. —Matthew 7:12

In May 2006, a man set out from base camp to make his third attempt on Mount Everest. He actually reached the summit, but on his way down he ran out of oxygen. As he lay on the side of the mountain dying, forty climbers passed him by.

Some say that at such oxygen-deprived altitudes, rescues are too perilous. But others say that climbers are too eager to reach the top and too selfish to help those in trouble.

I wonder what would have happened if someone who passed that stricken climber had said, "I will treat him the way I want to be treated." (MW)

PERSEVERANCE

WHEN YOU COME TO THE END OF YOUR ROPE,
TIE A KNOT AND HANG ON.
—FRANKLIN D. ROOSEVELT

Too Soon to Quit

Let us lay aside every weight, and the sin which so easily ensnares us, and let us run with endurance the race that is set before us. —Hebrews 12:1

Chris Couch was only sixteen years old when he first qualified to play golf at its highest level on the PGA Tour. He was quickly declared the next golfing prodigy and a surefire success for years to come.

Life, however, turned out to be more of a grind. Chris did not enjoy a sprint to success but endured a marathon that would take sixteen years and three different stints on "mini-tours." Tempted to quit, he persevered and finally, at age thirty-two, became a Tour winner for the first time when he captured the New Orleans Open in a thrilling finish. His perseverance paid off! (BC)

In Its Time

He has made everything beautiful in its time.   —*Ecclesiastes 3:11*

At age thirty she was ready to give up. She wrote in her diary, "My God, what will become of me? I have no desire but to die." But the dark clouds of despair gave way to the light, and in time she discovered a new purpose for living. When she died at age ninety, she had left her mark on history. Some believe that she and those who introduced antiseptics and chloroform to medicine did more than anyone to relieve human suffering in the nineteenth century. Her name was Florence Nightingale, founder of the nursing profession. (MD)

Hold the Line

Then He spoke a parable to them, that men always ought to pray and not lose heart.   —*Luke 18:1*

A wealthy woman phoned the manager of a concert hall and asked, "Have you found a diamond pendant? I think I lost it in your building last night."

The manager replied, "No, we haven't found it, but we'll look. Please hold the line."

During a quick search, the valuable diamond was located. When the manager returned to the phone, however, the woman was no longer on the line. She had hung up. She never called again, and the expensive jewelry went unclaimed.

We would fault that woman for her impatience and lack of persistence, but we sometimes act just like that when we pray. And in doing so, we give up something much more precious than diamonds. (PVG)

PRAYER

WE HAVE TO PRAY WITH OUR EYES ON GOD, NOT ON
THE DIFFICULTIES. —OSWALD CHAMBERS

Stand Up!

Be my rock of refuge, a fortress of defense to save me. —Psalm 31:2

In late January 1956, during the tense days of the Montgomery Boycott, civil rights leader Dr. Martin Luther King Jr. could not sleep. A threatening phone call had terrified him. So he prayed, "I am here taking a stand for what I believe is right. But Lord, I must confess that I'm weak now, I'm faltering. I'm losing my courage. Now, I am afraid... The people are looking to me for leadership, and if I stand before them without strength and courage, they too will falter. I am at the end of my powers... I can't face it alone."

Dr. King later wrote, "At that moment I experienced the presence of the Divine as I never experienced Him before. It seemed as though I could hear the quiet assurance of an inner voice saying, 'Stand up for righteousness, stand up for truth; and God will be at your side forever.' Almost at once my fears began to go. My uncertainty disappeared. I was ready to face anything." (DE)

"Hello, It's Me"

Vindicate me, O Lord, for I have walked in my integrity.
—*Psalm 26:1*

As Julie Ackerman Link was moving her laptop, cell phone, and assorted books and papers from one room to another, the "regular" phone rang. She hurriedly set down her stuff and rushed to answer the call before the answering machine kicked in. "Hello," she said. No reply. She said hello again when she heard rustling, but still no response. So she hung up and went back to her stuff on the floor. When she picked up her cell phone, she realized that she had accidentally speed-dialed her home phone number!

Julie laughed at herself, but then wondered: How often are my prayers more like calling myself than calling on God? (JAL)

A Time for Action

The Lord said to Moses, "Why do you cry to Me? Tell the children of Israel to go forward."
—*Exodus 14:15*

The woman chuckled as she told about the time she woke her husband to tell him she was in labor and needed to go to the hospital. He jumped out of bed, dropped to his knees, and said, "Honey, let's pray." She told him that it was not the time to kneel and pray. It was time to get dressed and head for the hospital. It was time for action! (HVL)

Worldwide Access

Through Him we both have access by one Spirit to the Father.
—*Ephesians 2:18*

When Mike Marolt is out of town, he remotely accesses the computer and files in his Aspen, Colorado, office. On a recent overseas trip, Marolt answered e-mails and kept in touch with his clients by using his laptop through a satellite phone hookup. This time, however, he was sitting in a base camp tent at 21,000 feet on the side of Mount Everest. These days even that doesn't surprise us because we have become used to the technology that provides access to the rest of the world anytime, anywhere.

We can easily develop a similar lack of amazement toward prayer. (DM)

Stagecoach Prayer

Whatever you ask in My name, that I will do, that the Father may be glorified in the Son. —*John 14:13*

Five-year-old Randy wanted a toy stagecoach for Christmas. While shopping with Mom, he found just the one he wanted. It was about six inches long and had cool wheels and dark brown plastic horses pulling it.

"Mommy, I want this one. Pleeeease!" he begged. As young children sometimes do, he threw a tantrum, insisting that he get that stagecoach for Christmas. Mom said, "We'll see," and took him home.

Randy was sure he'd get what he asked for. Christmas morning came, and he opened the package confidently. Sure enough, it was the stagecoach he had begged for. He was so pleased. But then his older brother said, "You really did a dumb thing to insist on getting that coach. Mom bought you a much bigger one, but when you begged for that little one, she exchanged it!" Suddenly the small stagecoach didn't seem so appealing. (AC)

Lost Prayers

In the day of my trouble I will call upon You, for You will answer me. —*Psalm 86:7*

The headline read: "Unanswered Prayers: Letters to God Found Dumped in Ocean."

The letters, three hundred in all and sent to a New Jersey minister, had been tossed in the ocean, most of them unopened. The minister was long dead. How the letters came to be floating in the surf off the New Jersey shore is a mystery.

The letters were addressed to the minister because he had promised to pray. Some of the letters asked for frivolous things; others were written by anguished spouses, children, or widows. They poured out their hearts to God, asking for help with relatives who were abusing drugs and alcohol, or spouses who were cheating on them. One asked God for a husband and father to love her child. The reporter concluded that all were "unanswered prayers."

But were they? (DR)

But Prayer

Constant prayer was offered to God for him by the church.
—Acts 12:5

When Herb Vander Lugt was a pastor, he often visited residents in rest homes. He tells about one dear elderly woman he met. She was blind and had been bedridden for seven years, yet she remained sweet and radiant.

One day she told Pastor Herb about a dream she had. She was in a beautiful garden where the grass was a luxuriant carpet beneath her and the fragrance of flowers filled the air. She dropped to her knees, entranced by the scene. As her thoughts were drawn heavenward, she felt the need to pray for her own pastor, for Pastor Herb, and for others. When she awakened, however, she discovered that she was still in her hospital bed.

With a smile she said to Pastor Herb, "You know, at first I was a bit disappointed. But in a sense the dream was true. This old bed has been a garden of prayer these seven years!"

Prayer had made her room a holy place of meditation and blessing. (HVL)

Instant Access

Let us draw near with a true heart in full assurance of faith.
—*Hebrews 10:22*

Pastor Rich McCarrell explained to his young son how his secretary screened his phone calls at the church office. "If your mom calls me and I'm busy, the church secretary will tell her what I'm doing, and then Mom will decide if I should be interrupted or if she should leave a message."

Then he said to his son, "If you call me, you'll be put right through. I want you to know that you can call me anytime, because you're my son."

A few days later, the church secretary put a call through to the pastor from his son. He said hello and asked what he could do for his son. The boy replied, "Nothing, Dad. I just wanted to make sure I could actually get through to you that easily." (AC)

Doing Our Part

I have heard your prayer... surely I will heal you. On the third day you shall go up to the house of the Lord.   —*2 Kings 20:5*

A runner at a school track meet crossed the finish line just ahead of his nearest rival. A bystander, noticing that the winner's lips were moving during the last couple of laps, wondered what he was saying. So he asked him about it.

"I was praying," the runner answered. Pointing to his feet, he said, "I was saying, 'You pick 'em up, Lord, and I'll put 'em down.'"

That athlete prayed for God's help, but he also did his part in answering his own prayer. (RD)

A Clear Call

Samuel answered, "Speak, for Your servant hears."

—1 Samuel 3:10

When George Washington Carver was a student at Iowa Agricultural College (now Iowa State University), he and a friend planned to go as missionaries to Africa. But as his agricultural studies progressed, Carver, a devout Christian, began to sense a different calling from God.

When Booker T. Washington asked him to join the faculty of Tuskegee Institute in Alabama, Carver made it a matter of earnest prayer.

In 1896, Carver wrote to Washington: "It has been the one ideal of my life to be of the greatest good to the greatest number of my people possible, and to this end I have been preparing myself for these many years." He pledged to do all he could through the power of Christ to better the conditions of African-Americans in the racially segregated South. (DM)

PRIDE

PRIDE GETS NO PLEASURE OUT OF HAVING SOMETHING, ONLY OUT OF HAVING MORE OF IT THAN THE NEXT MAN. —C. S. LEWIS

No Strings Attached

Humble yourselves in the sight of the Lord, and He will lift you up.

—James 4:10

In the library of Pastor Howard Sugden was a well-worn book containing the works of John Newton. Inside was a poem titled "The Kite; or Pride Must Have a Fall." The kite in Newton's poem dreamed of being cut free from its string:

"Were I but free, I'd take a flight,
And pierce the clouds beyond their sight,
But, ah! Like a poor pris'ner bound,
My string confines me near the ground."

The kite does finally manage to tug itself free, but instead of soaring higher in the sky, it crashes into the sea.

It is our willingness to be humbled (or held down) that God uses to lift us up. (JAL)

RECONCILIATION

Apology Hotline

Leave your gift there before the altar, and go your way. First be reconciled to your brother, and then come and offer your gift.
—*Matthew 5:24*

Jesse Jacobs has created an apology hotline that makes it possible to apologize without actually talking to the person you've wronged. People who are unable or unwilling to unburden their conscience in person call the hotline and leave a message on an answering machine. Each week, thirty to fifty calls are logged, as people apologize for things from adultery to embezzlement.

"The hotline offers participants a chance to alleviate their guilt and, to some degree, to own up to their misdeeds," said Jacobs.

The apology hotline may seem to offer some relief from guilt, but this is not how Jesus instructed His followers to handle conflict. In the Sermon on the Mount, Jesus told us to deal with conflict by taking the initiative and going to the offended brother or sister to apologize for the offense. The Master encouraged His followers to be reconciled with one another eagerly, aggressively, quickly, and personally. (MW)

RESOLUTIONS

RESOLVE TO PERFORM WHAT YOU OUGHT;
PERFORM WITHOUT FAIL WHAT YOU RESOLVE.
—BENJAMIN FRANKLIN

A Sense of Purpose

[They] entered into... an oath to walk in God's Law... and to observe and do all the commandments of the Lord our Lord.
—Nehemiah 10:29

In 1722, Jonathan Edwards drew up a list of seventy resolutions, dedicating himself to live in harmony with God and others. The following resolutions give a picture of the serious purpose with which Edwards approached his relationship with God. He resolved:

- To do whatever is most to God's glory.
- To do my duty for the good of mankind in general.
- Never to do anything which I should be afraid to do if it were the last hour of my life.
- To study the Scriptures steadily, constantly, and frequently.
- To ask myself at the end of every day, week, month, and year if I could possibly have done better.
- Until I die, not to act as if I were my own, but entirely and altogether God's. (MW)

Plugging Away

I cling to Your testimonies; O Lord, do not put me to shame! I will run the course of Your commandments. *—Psalm 119:31–32*

Samuel Johnson, a deeply committed Christian who lived in the eighteenth century, frequently wrote resolutions in his journals.

Here is a typical entry: "I have corrected no external habits, nor kept any of the resolutions made in the beginning of the year, yet I hope still to be reformed, and not to lose my whole life in idle purposes." (VG)

RESURRECTION

THE ENTIRE PLAN FOR THE FUTURE HAS ITS KEY IN THE RESURRECTION. —BILLY GRAHAM

Jordan's Idea

All Scripture is given by inspiration of God, and is profitable for doctrine, for reproof, for correction, for instruction in righteousness. —2 Timothy 3:16

One spring day, Jordan began asking questions about Jesus' resurrection as his mom was taking him to preschool. Realizing that her son thought Jesus was rising from the dead for the first time this Easter, she tried to correct him. She pulled the car over and told him all about Jesus' death and resurrection. She concluded, "Jesus rose from the dead a long time ago, and now He wants to live in our hearts."

But Jordan still didn't understand.

Unsure how she could make it any clearer, she said, "How about if we stop by the bookstore? I saw some books about Easter when I was there last week. We'll get one and read through it together."

With a wisdom beyond his years, Jordan responded, "Can't we just read the Bible?" (AC)

Fact, Not Fable

If Christ is not risen, your faith is futile; you are still in your sins!
—1 Corinthians 15:17

The resurrection of Jesus Christ is the cornerstone of the Christian faith. Without it we have no hope for this life or for the life to come. That's why it is important to recognize that our belief in Christ's resurrection is not based on some religious feeling, nor on unfounded rumor, but on historical fact with solid evidence to support it.

In the early part of the twentieth century, a group of lawyers met in England to discuss the biblical accounts of Jesus' resurrection. They wanted to see if enough information was available to make a case that would hold up in a court of law. They concluded that Christ's resurrection was one of the most well-established facts of history!

In his book *Countdown,* G. B. Hardy offers thought-provoking questions about the resurrection: "There are but two essential requirements: (1) Has anyone cheated death and proved it? (2) Is it available to me? Here is the complete record: Confucius' tomb—occupied. Buddha's tomb—occupied. Muhammad's tomb—occupied. Jesus' tomb—empty! Argue as you will, there is no point in following a loser." (DE)

Dirty Windows

If we believe that Jesus died and rose again, even so God will bring with Him those who sleep in Jesus.   *—1 Thessalonians 4:14*

The Shepherd's Home in Wisconsin has a problem with dirty windows. Although many of its residents are severely disabled, they love Jesus and understand that He has promised to return someday and give them new bodies. "Every day," said the superintendent, "some of them go to the windows and press their noses against the glass, looking for Him."

The expectation of those precious people is genuine. Their irreversible mental and physical limitations fuel their longing for the day when they will be perfectly whole and free. (DD)

Empty Proof

He rose again the third day according to the Scriptures.

—*1 Corinthians 15:4*

In the days after the French Revolution, a man tried to start a new religion that he believed was superior to Christianity. But he was disappointed at his lack of success. He revealed his frustration to a clergyman and asked what he could do.

The clergyman replied that it was no easy task to begin a new religion—so difficult that he had nothing to suggest. But after a moment's reflection, he said, "There's one plan that you might want to consider. Why don't you get yourself crucified and rise again the third day?"

The firm foundation of the Christian faith is an empty tomb. (HR)

Incredible

Why should it be thought incredible by you that God raises the dead? —*Acts 26:8*

Resurrection is not an incredible, irrational idea. We can see illustrations of resurrection all around us in nature. For example, Egyptian garden peas that had been buried for three thousand years were brought out and planted on June 4, 1844. Within a few days they had germinated and broken the ground. Buried for three thousand years—then resurrected. That's amazing!

If God could take some dust and breathe life into it to create a man, why would anyone think it incredible for this same God to raise someone from the dead? (MD)

SACRIFICE

HE'S NO FOOL WHO GIVES UP WHAT HE CANNOT KEEP
TO GAIN WHAT HE CANNOT LOSE. —JIM ELLIOT

At Risk

I could wish that I myself were accursed from Christ for my brethren, my countrymen according to the flesh. —Romans 9:3

In the film *The Guardian,* the viewer is taken into the world of United States Coast Guard rescue swimmers. Eighteen weeks of intense training prepares these courageous men and women for the task of jumping from helicopters to rescue those in danger at sea. The challenges they face include hypothermia and death by drowning.

Why would people risk so much for strangers? The answer is found in the rescue swimmer's motto, "So Others May Live." (BC)

Total Giving

She out of her poverty put in all that she had. —Mark 12:44

"Mr. Branon, I have to talk with you about something really important," said the voice on the other end of the line. It was two days before a small group of teens and adults were to leave for Jamaica on a special missions trip. The group had been planning for months to go to a school for deaf children to build a much-needed playground. So when this teen called, Dave Branon thought, *Oh, no. She can't go.*

But when the girl, her mom, and Dave met for lunch that day, she told him she was donating her entire savings to help pay for the trip—money she had been saving to buy a car.

"As I was praying the past couple of nights," she explained, "I felt that God was telling me to give all of my money."

That day the three of them had tears of joy with their burgers and fries. (DB)

Doing Well

If you really fulfill the royal law according to the Scripture, "You shall love your neighbor as yourself," you do well. —James 2:8

In the book *Flags of Our Fathers,* James Bradley recounts the World War II battle of Iwo Jima and its famous flag-raising on Mount Suribachi. Bradley's father, John, was one of the flag-raisers. But more important, he was a Navy corpsman—a medic.

In the heat of battle, facing a barrage of bullets from both sides, Bradley exposed himself to danger so he could care for the wounded and dying. This self-sacrifice showed his willingness and determination to care for others, even though it meant placing himself at great personal risk.

Doc Bradley won the Navy Cross for his heroism and valor, but he never spoke of it to his family. In fact, it was only after his death that they learned of his military decorations. To Doc, it wasn't about winning medals; it was about caring for his buddies. (BC)

SALVATION

SALVATION IS THE WORK OF GOD FOR MAN; IT IS NOT
THE WORK OF MAN FOR GOD.
—LEWIS SPERRY CHAFER

Lincoln's Faith

Ought not the Christ to have suffered these things and to enter into His glory? —Luke 24:26

Abraham Lincoln was a backwoodsman who rose from humble beginnings to the heights of political power. During the dark days of the U.S. Civil War, he served as a compassionate and resolute president. Depression and mental pain were his frequent companions. Yet the terrible emotional suffering he endured drove him to receive Jesus Christ by faith.

Lincoln told a crowd in his hometown in Illinois: "When I left Springfield, I asked the people to pray for me; I was not a Christian. When I buried my son, the severest trial of my life, I was not a Christian. But when I saw the graves of thousands of our soldiers, I then and there consecrated myself to Christ. I do love Jesus."

Life's most painful tragedies can bring us to a deeper understanding of the Savior. (DF)

Big Changes

Therefore, if anyone is in Christ, he is a new creation; old things have passed away; behold, all things have become new.
—*2 Corinthians 5:17*

Tremendous changes occur when a person becomes a new creature in Christ. Evangelist D. L. Moody enumerated the major points in that life-altering transaction and wrote them on the flyleaf of his Bible.

1. Justification: a change of standing—before God.
2. Regeneration: a change of nature—from God.
3. Repentance: a change of mind—about God.
4. Conversion: a change of life—for God.
5. Adoption: a change of family—in God.
6. Sanctification: a change of service—to God.
7. Glorification: a change of place—with God. (HB)

Blood Exchange

Much more then, having now been justified by His blood, we shall be saved from wrath through Him. —*Romans 5:9*

When Lily Pinneo, a missionary nurse, was in West Africa, she contracted a deadly disease called Lassa fever. After Lily was flown to New York for medical treatment, her temperature soared to 107°F. To reduce the fever, doctors packed her in ice and fed her intravenously. The fever subsided. After nine weeks, she had lost twenty-eight pounds and most of her hair. Yet somehow, she survived.

In a laboratory, Dr. Casals carefully isolated and analyzed the Lassa virus. But he too fell ill from his exposure to the disease. At the time, no known treatment was effective. Fortunately, Nurse Pinneo was convalescing and had built up antibodies to the dread disease. She donated blood plasma to Dr. Casals and he recovered too. Her blood saved his life. (DF)

Celebrate Freedom

The law of the Spirit of life in Christ Jesus has made me free from the law of sin and death.　　　　　　　　　—Romans 8:2

After being kidnapped, held hostage for thirteen days, and released, New Zealand news cameraman Olaf Wiig, with a broad smile on his face, announced, "I feel more alive now than I have in my entire life."

For reasons difficult to understand, being freed is more exhilarating than being free. (JAL)

Which Way?

The message of the cross is foolishness to those who are perishing.　　　　　　　　　—1 Corinthians 1:18

Every night, Howard and Mel frequented the cheap bars in Grand Rapids, Michigan, hoping to drink away another miserable day. Finally, the pain of a wasted life was too much, so Mel hopped a train for Chicago, where he hoped to end it all.

But as he walked barefoot through a Chicago snowstorm in 1897, heading for a self-imposed demise in Lake Michigan, he was stopped by a worker from the Pacific Garden Mission. Mel went inside, heard the gospel, and accepted Christ as his Savior.

Later, Mel went back to Grand Rapids to start a mission. Howard heard that his drinking buddy was saved and sober.

But instead of trusting Jesus for himself, Howard just laughed at "Old Mel." To him, "the message of the cross [was] foolishness." Finally, the drinking took its toll on Howard, and he committed suicide.

More than one hundred years later, the Mel Trotter Mission still welcomes people who need a place to stay and who need Jesus. And one hundred years later, writer Dave Branon concludes, his family is still saddened by Howard's demise. You see, Howard was his wife's grandfather. (DB)

Truth Seekers

I will never forget Your precepts, for by them You have given me life. —Psalm 119:93

The young woman's quest for God began when she was eleven years old and living under atheistic communism in the former Soviet Union. That's when she saw some artwork that depicted the baby Jesus. When she heard that this represented what authorities called a "myth" about God sending His Son to earth, she began to seek the truth.

She also heard that God had written a book of His truth, and she searched for a copy. It wasn't until she was almost thirty years old that she finally found a Bible she was permitted to read. At last she had the information she needed to trust Jesus as Savior.

From 1971 to 1989, this young woman risked her own safety to search for the truth of God's Word. Today she is a lawyer who works to protect her fellow Russian citizens from religious persecution. The message of God's love in Christ is spreading because this one woman was a truth seeker. (DB)

Good Enough?

Though your sins are like scarlet, they shall be as white as snow.
—Isaiah 1:18

A friend told *ODB* writer David Roper about a young mother who was trying to explain her father's death to her four-year-old. The girl wondered where Grandpa was.

"I'm sure he's in heaven," the mother answered, "because he was very good."

The girl replied sadly, "I guess I won't be in heaven."

"Why not?" her mother asked in surprise.

"'Cause I'm not very good."

The story saddened David, as he is always saddened when he hears of those who believe they must be very good to get into heaven, especially since we all know deep down in our hearts that we're not very good at all. (DR)

Arriving Late

The last will be first, and the first last.   —Matthew 20:16

Eddie, an outspoken atheist, spent his entire life denying the existence of God. Then, at age fifty, he contracted a debilitating disease, and his health slowly deteriorated. As he lay in a hospice house awaiting death, Eddie was visited almost every day by some Christian friends he had known in high school. They told him again of Christ's love. But the closer Eddie came to dying, the more it appeared he was not interested in God.

Then, one Sunday, a pastor stopped by to visit. To everyone's surprise, Eddie prayed with him and asked Jesus for forgiveness and salvation. A few weeks later, he died.

Eddie denied Christ for almost fifty years and spent just two weeks loving and trusting Him. But because of his faith, he will experience forever God's presence, glory, love, majesty, and perfection. Some may argue that this isn't fair. But according to Jesus' parable in Matthew 20, it's not about fairness. It's about God's goodness and grace. (DB)

No Greater Lover

Greater love has no one than this, than to lay down one's life for his friends.   —*John 15:13*

Melbourne, Australia, is home to the Shrine of Remembrance, a war memorial honoring those who died for their country. Built following World War I, it has since been expanded to honor those who served in subsequent conflicts.

It's a beautiful place, with reminders of courage and devotion, but the highlight of the shrine is a hall containing a carved stone that simply reads, "Greater Love Hath No Man." Every year on the eleventh day of the eleventh month at 11:00 a.m. a mirror reflects the sun's light onto the stone to spotlight the word *love*. It is a poignant tribute to those who gave their lives.

We honor the memory of those who paid the ultimate price for freedom. Yet the words on that stone carry a far greater meaning. Jesus spoke them the night before He died on the cross for the sins of a needy world. (BC)

Is Jesus Exclusive?

Jesus said to him, "I am the way, the truth, and the life. No one comes to the Father except through Me."   —*John 14:6*

Billy Graham's daughter Anne Graham Lotz appeared on a popular news talk program. The interviewer asked, "Are you one of those who believe that Jesus is exclusively the only way to heaven?" He added, "You know how mad that makes people these days!"

Without blinking she replied, "Jesus is not exclusive. He died so that anyone could come to Him for salvation." (JS)

Running for Nothing

Nor is there salvation in any other, for there is no other name under heaven given among men by which we must be saved. —*Acts 4:12*

As Roger Weber started the 2006 Chicago Marathon, he noticed something on the ground. It was a runner's chip—the device each runner puts on his or her shoe to record progress electronically at various timing stations during the race. Apparently one poor runner would be traversing the next 26.2 miles on foot with nothing to show for it.

Officially that runner did not run the race. There was no record of his participation. Even if he finished the race in record time, it wouldn't matter. The folks who organize the race set the rules, and no matter how well someone runs, if the officials say the runner doesn't qualify, that's the way it is.

In one sense, that's also the way it is with all of us. We can run what appears to be a good race (a good life) by doing good things for others and obeying lots of rules. But when we arrive at the final checkpoint—heaven—and haven't made sure our name is recorded in the Lamb's Book of Life by putting our faith in Jesus as our Savior, we are disqualified to enter. (DB)

I Smile

If anyone is in Christ, he is a new creation; old things have passed away; behold, all things have become new. —*2 Corinthians 5:17*

A few years ago, singer Russ Lee came out with a song titled "I Smile." When you discover how his life was changed by Jesus Christ, you'll know why he sings a song that says, "I smile when I think about the way You turned my life around. I smile when I think about the happiness in You I've found."

When Russ was seventeen, his days were wasted on drugs, alcohol, boredom, and pain. His life was full of self-inflicted trouble and hopelessness. One day, while listening to an old rock song called "I Can't Get No Satisfaction," he realized that this described his life. Two days later, a friend invited him to church. There Russ heard that real satisfaction comes from knowing Jesus Christ, so he reached out in faith to Him.

So, what was the first thing Russ did after trusting Christ? According to the book *Touched by the Savior* by Mike Yorkey, Russ said, "I walked back out to my car. In the trunk was a garbage bag filled with drugs I had been selling. *I won't be needing these again*, I thought, and I was right. I threw the bag away. From that day forward, God transformed my life from the inside out. I became a new creation." (DB)

SANCTIFICATION

GOD PRESERVES THE SAINTS, BUT HE DOES NOT
PICKLE THEM. —VANCE HAVNER

Under Construction

To Him who is able to keep you from stumbling, and to present you faultless before the presence of His glory with exceeding joy.
—Jude 1:24

Years ago, Ruth Bell Graham, wife of evangelist Billy Graham, saw a sign by the road: "End of Construction—Thank you for your patience." Smiling, she remarked that she wanted those words on her gravestone.

After her death in June 2007, her desire was carried out. Her grave marker bears the Chinese character for righteousness (Mrs. Graham was born in China), followed by the words that made her smile. (DM)

Forever Perfect

By one offering He has perfected forever those who are being sanctified.
                                                    —*Hebrews 10:14*

When *Our Daily Bread* writer Albert Lee first heard of Sara Lee cakes, the brand name caught his attention because one of the most common Asian family names is "Lee." Being a Chinese Lee himself, he wondered if Sara was Chinese or Korean.

Then he learned that Charlie Lubin, an American bakery entrepreneur, had named his cheesecakes after his daughter Sara Lee. Sara said her father wanted this product to be "perfect because he was naming it after me." (AL)

Christ—Our Everything

You are in Christ Jesus, who became for us wisdom from God—and righteousness and sanctification and redemption.
                                                    —*1 Corinthians 1:30*

Thomas Shepard (1605–1649) was raised in a godly Puritan home, but while he was attending Cambridge University he fell into a life of sin. One Sunday morning when he awoke from a drunken stupor, a heavy weight of sadness over the enormity of his guilt crushed him to the point that he left his former way of life.

For the next nine months, the fear of God's wrath almost drove him to "run my head against walls . . . and kill myself." But while listening to a sermon on 1 Corinthians 1:30, he suddenly realized that Christ was everything he needed—that Jesus had lived the perfect life he couldn't live, had paid for his sins on the cross, and was now his Advocate in heaven.

Commenting on John 1:12, "As many as received Him, to them He gave the right to become children of God," Shepard wrote, "The Lord gave me a heart to receive Christ with a naked hand . . . and so the Lord gave me peace." (HVL)

New Creatures in Christ

Therefore, if anyone is in Christ, he is a new creation; old things have passed away; behold, all things have become new.

—2 Corinthians 5:17

An English clergyman was the guest at a girls' school while visiting some mission stations in the South Sea Islands. He was profoundly impressed by the spiritual concern of the students, by the art that decorated their buildings, and by their personal cleanliness. But the highlight came as he boarded the ship to return to England. The girls lined up in two rows and sang enthusiastically, "What a wonderful change in my life has been wrought, since Jesus came into my heart!" He was deeply touched, especially when one of the staff members whispered, "Every one of those girls is either the daughter or the granddaughter of a cannibal!" (HB)

SATAN

HE WHO TAKES HIS STAND FOR CHRIST IS NOT LIKELY
TO FALL FOR THE DEVIL. —AUTHOR UNKNOWN

Fooled by Thunderbolt

Satan himself transforms himself into an angel of light.

—2 Corinthians 11:14

When an English robber called Captain Thunderbolt escaped the law and moved to the eastern U.S. in 1818, he took on the name Dr. John Wilson and began practicing medicine. Often he wore three suits of clothes to escape recognition by making himself look larger and covering up a deformed leg.

Just before the man died, he asked his friends to bury him without removing his clothes. But to prepare his body for proper burial, that request could not be honored. The mortician was surprised to find scars from wounds and a withered leg. A search of "Dr. Wilson's" house revealed a stash of watches, jewelry, and diamonds, and the sheriff learned that the doctor was in fact Thunderbolt, a thief in disguise. They had been fooled!

Satan too can fool us into thinking he's someone he is not. (AC)

Satan's Secret

He who is in you is greater than he who is in the world.
—1 John 4:4

A driving instructor in Germany was stopped by police after a minor accident with a truck. When asked for his driver's license, he couldn't provide one. He had been instructing students for more than forty years on how to drive, yet he didn't have his own license! Years earlier, he had failed a driving test, and he was fearful of trying again. He kept this fact a secret out of embarrassment.

Likewise, Satan has a secret he doesn't want us to know: He doesn't have the power to separate us from God. (AC)

Shrike System

Be sober, be vigilant; because your adversary the devil walks about like a roaring lion, seeking whom he may devour.   —1 Peter 5:8

The ancient sport of falconry used trained hawks or falcons in the pursuit of wild game. When the "educated predator" was allowed to fly, however, it often rose too high for human eyes to see. So a hunter often carried a small caged bird called a shrike. By watching the antics of the little bird, the man could always tell where his hawk was, for the shrike instinctively feared the predator and cocked its head to keep it in view.

Christians desperately need an alert perception similar to that of the shrike to detect their spiritual enemy. (MD)

SERVICE

THE BEST AND PERHAPS MOST EFFECTIVE LEADERSHIP IS
THAT FOUNDED IN SERVICE. —JACOB MURRAY

Reception Surprise

Through love serve one another. —*Galatians 5:13*

When Cristine Bouwkamp and Kyle Kramer got married in the spring of 2007, they did something most of us wouldn't think of doing. Instead of hosting a "sit-down dinner," they held a simple reception at the church and invited their guests to help distribute food to people in need.

They bought a truckload of food and had it delivered to the church parking lot. Then they and their wedding guests served the people of the neighborhood.

Cristine and Kyle said the first thing they wished to do as a married couple was to serve others. Because God had changed their lives so radically, they wanted to "bless God for blessing us with each other." (AC)

Bible Guy

Having then gifts differing according to the grace that is given to us, let us use them. —*Romans 12:6*

When the youth group in Rich's church needed Bibles for study, he went on a search for more than seventy copies. He got what the group needed, but he never stopped collecting and distributing Bibles.

People and businesses donate money; others give him new and used Bibles to share. The motto on the side of the van he uses for this ministry explains his simple desire: "Need a Bible? Ask me for one."

Rich is an ordinary guy, a heating and plumbing technician, who carries on this ministry in his spare time. His nickname around his church is "the Bible guy." (AC)

Giving to Get

Let us not grow weary while doing good, for in due season we shall reap if we do not lose heart. —Galatians 6:9

Years ago, Dr. Wilfred Grenfell served as a medical missionary in Labrador. On a recruiting tour, he challenged nurses at Johns Hopkins Hospital to join him for a summer in his difficult ministry. He promised them hardship and discomfort. He warned that instead of earning a salary, they would have to pay their own expenses. But he also promised them they would experience joy because "it's having the time of anyone's life to be in the service of Christ."

A nurse who accepted that challenge wrote this after her return from Labrador: "I never knew before that life was good for anything but what one could get out of it. Now I know that the real fun lies in seeing how much one can put into life for others." (VG)

Don't Row

That He would grant you, according to the riches of His glory, to be strengthened with might through His Spirit in the inner man. —Ephesians 3:16

During a picnic on a scorching day at a Wisconsin lake, Ole's fiancée Bess said how much she would enjoy some ice cream. So the young Norwegian immigrant gladly made a five-mile round-trip by rowboat to bring it to her.

When he returned exhausted with a container of melted ice cream, Ole told himself there must be a better way. He put his mechanical mind to work, and a year later, in 1907, Ole Evinrude field-tested his lightweight, detachable motor for small boats. He married Bess, and when the outboard motors went into commercial production, she wrote the advertising slogan: "Don't Row! Throw the Oars Away!"

Ole Evinrude was not a lazy man, but he understood the limits of human power. Each day we employ machinery to accomplish the tasks of life. But we often stubbornly rely on ourselves when we're trying to serve God. (DM)

Garbage Detail

All of you be submissive to one another, and be clothed with humility.
—1 Peter 5:5

Richard De Haan told the story about how it was once his privilege to preach in a church where love and warmth were especially evident. He was impressed by the members' willingness to pitch in and work. On the Sunday Richard spoke, three services were scheduled. The women of the church provided a bountiful meal that was served between the services for visitors who had traveled a long distance.

Following the dinner, after most of the people had left, Richard noticed a distinguished-looking couple clearing the tables and dumping the paper plates into large plastic bags. When he complimented them on what they were doing, they said matter-of-factly, "Oh, we're 'the garbage detail.' We volunteered to clean up after every church function. We consider it a ministry."

Richard De Haan concluded: How wonderful that this man and woman were not only available to serve the Lord, but they humbly did what others might consider demeaning work. These dear people were glad to be what they cheerfully called "the garbage detail." (RD)

SIN AND CONFESSION

Clean It Up

When a man or woman commits any sin... against the Lord... then he shall confess the sin which he has committed. —Numbers 5:6–7

Researchers at the University of Toronto reported in 2006 that people who are suffering from a guilty conscience experience "a powerful urge to wash themselves." To study this effect, the researchers asked volunteers to recall past sins. They were then given an opportunity to wash their hands as a symbol of cleansing their conscience. Those who had recalled their sins washed their hands at "twice the rate of study subjects who had not imagined past transgressions." (MW)

Here Comes the Boss

If we confess our sins, He is faithful and just to forgive us our sins and to cleanse us from all unrighteousness. —1 John 1:9

A number of computer games come with a special feature called the "Boss Key." If you're playing a game when you're supposed to be working, and someone (like the boss) walks into your office, you quickly strike the Boss Key. Your computer screen changes immediately, hiding what you've been doing.

Trying to hide from others when we've done something wrong comes naturally. We may feel guilty, but our desire to avoid admitting our responsibility is often stronger than our guilt. (AC)

Pointing Fingers

There is none who does good, no, not one. —Psalm 14:3

An employee in the bill collection department of a large store gives us an insight into human nature. He says that he repeatedly gets the following response from customers who are delinquent in paying their bills: "I know you must have others who owe a lot more than I do. Get off my back, will you!"

The employee further says, "They miss the point entirely. Sure, there are a lot of others who owe more. But somehow I have to tell them in a nice way, 'Look, what somebody else owes isn't the issue. Our records say that your account is overdue!'"

The tendency of sinful man has always been to shift attention from himself by pointing the finger at others. (MD)

Sowing and Reaping

Do not be deceived, God is not mocked; for whatever a man sows, that he will also reap. —Galatians 6:7

Bill Crowder tells this story on himself from his high school days.

It seemed innocent enough at the time. I had just come home from school and told my mom that I was going to a friend's house to play football. She insisted that I stay home and do my homework. Instead, I slipped out the back door and spent the next two hours making tackles and touchdowns in my friend's backyard. But on the last play, I was tackled into a swing-set and knocked out my front tooth. It hurt like crazy, but not as badly as telling my parents.

That choice to disobey put me on a ten-year path of dental problems and pain that have continuing implications today. As ballplayer Roy Hobbs said in the film *The Natural*, "Some mistakes you never stop paying for." (BC)

If Doubtful, Don't

He who doubts is condemned if he eats, because he does not eat from faith; for whatever is not from faith is sin. —Romans 14:23

In his book *Illustrations of Bible Truth,* H. A. Ironside tells about a man who was getting ready to attend a banquet. He wanted to put on a white shirt he had worn on a previous occasion, so he was inspecting it carefully to see if it was too dirty. His wife noticed what he was doing and called out, "Remember, Dear, if it's doubtful, don't." The issue was settled. The man threw the shirt into the laundry hamper.

That's a principle that can be applied to questionable matters of conscience. If it's doubtful, don't. (RD)

You Won't Get Away with It

Our transgressions are multiplied before You, and our sins testify against us. —Isaiah 59:12

A group of students at Renaissance High School in Detroit decided to cut classes to attend a rock concert in Hart Plaza. They felt they had gotten away with it, but the next day when the *Detroit News* appeared on the newsstand, it carried a color photo of the concert—on the front page. And who was in that picture? The delinquent students of Renaissance High, easily recognizable by anyone.

The Bible teaches that we cannot hide our iniquities. (DE)

The Pretender

Confess your trespasses to one another, and pray for one another, that you may be healed. —James 5:16

When a waitress in Ohio asked to see a customer's driver's license, she was shocked when she saw the photo on the ID. It was her own picture! The waitress had lost her driver's license a month earlier, and this young woman was using it so she'd have "proof" she was old enough to drink alcohol.

The police were called, and the customer was arrested for identity theft. Trying to gain what she wanted, she pretended to be someone she wasn't.

Some people put on a false front in other ways. They pretend they "have it all together" to gain the approval of others. But inside they're struggling with brokenness, guilt, doubt, or an addiction or other persistent sin.

Admit that you aren't perfect. Then seek the counsel of a godly brother or sister in Christ. (AC)

The Power of Sin

Let us lay aside every weight, and the sin which so easily ensnares us.
—Hebrews 12:1

Bill Crowder was having lunch with a pastor friend when the discussion sadly turned to a mutual friend in ministry who had failed morally. As the two of them grieved together over this fallen comrade, now out of ministry, Bill wondered aloud, "I know anyone can be tempted and anyone can stumble, but he's a smart guy. How could he think he could get away with it?"

Without blinking, his friend responded, "Sin makes us stupid." (BC)

The Nature of the Beast

I know that in me (that is, in my flesh) nothing good dwells; for to will is present with me, but how to perform what is good I do not find. *—Romans 7:18*

Years ago, Mart De Haan says, his family had a pet raccoon named Jason. One minute Jason would snuggle up on your lap like a perfect angel and the next he'd be engaged in the most fiendish antics. If unrestrained, he would raid the garbage can or tear up the flowerbed. Although he was a delightful pet, the De Haans became increasingly aware that his destructive actions were governed by his wild instincts. Jason would always have the nature of a raccoon, and the family had to watch him closely, no matter how tame he seemed to be.

Mart says that when he observed Jason's behavior, he thought of the sinful nature that we as Christians retain even though we are indwelt by the Holy Spirit. (MD)

Foolish Baggage

Let us lay aside every weight, and the sin which so easily ensnares us.
—Hebrews 12:1

In 1845, the ill-fated Franklin Expedition sailed from England to find a passage across the Arctic Ocean.

The crew loaded their two sailing ships with a lot of things they didn't need: a 1,200-volume library, fine china, crystal goblets, and sterling silverware for each officer with his initials engraved on the handles. Amazingly, though, each ship took only a twelve-day supply of coal for their auxiliary steam engines.

The ships became trapped in vast frozen plains of ice. After several months, Lord Franklin died. The men decided to trek to safety in small groups, but none of them survived.

One story is especially heartbreaking. Two officers pulled a large sled more than sixty-five miles across the treacherous ice. When rescuers found their bodies, they discovered that the sled was filled with table silver.

The men of the Franklin Expedition contributed to their own demise by carrying what they didn't need. But we sometimes do the same. We drag baggage through life that we don't need. Evil thoughts that hinder us. Bad habits that drag us down. Grudges that we won't let go.

Let's determine to "lay aside every weight, and the sin which so easily ensnares us." (DE)

Catch and Release

Jesus answered them, "Most assuredly, I say to you, whoever commits sin is a slave of sin."   —*John 8:34*

David Roper is a "catch and release" fisherman, which means he doesn't kill the trout he catches. He nets them and handles them gently and sets them free. It's a technique that ensures "sustainability," as conservation officers like to say, and keeps trout and other target species from disappearing in heavily fished waters.

"I rarely release a trout without recalling Paul's words about those who have been 'taken captive' by Satan to do his will (2 Timothy 2:26)," Roper says, "for I know that our adversary the Devil does not catch and release but captures to consume and destroy."

We may think we can deliberately sin in a limited way for a short period of time and then get ourselves free. But as Jesus teaches us, "Whoever commits sin is a slave of sin." (DR)

Starting Over

If anyone is in Christ, he is a new creation; old things have passed away; behold, all things have become new.   —*2 Corinthians 5:17*

The little boy looked up at his mother and asked, "Mama, do you know why God made us?"

Knowing that her son had his own explanation, she asked, "Well, Justin, do *you* know why?"

"Oh, that's easy. Because the people in the Bible were so bad, He wanted to start over." (DB)

SPIRITUAL GIFTS

SPIRITUAL GIFTS ARE MEANT TO BE USED, NOT MERELY
ADMIRED. —AUTHOR UNKNOWN

What Good Is a Rubber Tree?

There are diversities of gifts, but the same Spirit. There are differences of ministries, but the same Lord. —1 Corinthians 12:4–5

On one of his voyages to the New World, Christopher Columbus came across a remarkable tree. It had round fruit that bounced like a ball. Its Indian name was *caoutchouc*—"the weeping wood."

The tree was given that name because it emitted a sap that looked like the tree's tears. Eventually, inventors discovered that the sap could be harvested and allowed to harden into an eraser that rubbed out pencil lead—hence the name "rubber."

In the 1830s it was found that rubber could withstand very cold temperatures when sulfur was added to it. This led the way to a huge demand for rubber when the automobile was invented. Later it was discovered that the sap could be used to make latex surgical gloves. The rubber tree had multiple uses that needed only to be discovered.

Likewise, when we consider the spiritual gifts described in the Bible, we may find that we have more than one. (DF)

The Tests of Criticism

Faithful are the wounds of a friend, but the kisses of an enemy are deceitful. —Proverbs 27:6

After a church service in which the minister had preached about spiritual gifts, he was greeted at the door by a woman who said, "Pastor, I believe I have the gift of criticism."

He responded, "Do you remember the person in Jesus' parable who had the one talent? Do you recall what he did with it?"

"Yes," replied the woman, "he went out and buried it" (see Matthew 25:18).

With a smile, the pastor suggested, "Go, and do likewise!" (RD)

Use Your Gifts

When He ascended on high, He led captivity captive, and gave gifts to men. —*Ephesians 4:8*

Dave Egner tells of reading in the *Detroit News* a humorous little story about Bill Cosby's aged mother that illustrates how useless gifts are unless they are used. She had been raised in poverty, and the family had very little money as Bill was growing up. As a result, she never had modern conveniences and had gotten accustomed to doing things the hard way. When the children were old enough to get jobs, they often gave their mother appliances as Christmas gifts to make her life easier. But she wouldn't use them.

Bill especially remembered that after a while his mother had two or three toasters. But she left them in their boxes and put them on top of the refrigerator. At breakfast she would still do the toast in the oven. If the boys protested, she would say, "Leave them on the refrigerator. I'm used to doing it the old way."

Some of us are like Bill Cosby's mother. Along with the precious gift of salvation, we have been given wonderful gifts from God—but we don't use them. (DE)

Bricklayers and Violinists

Having then gifts differing according to the grace that is given to us, let us use them. —*Romans 12:6*

A concert violinist had a brother who was a bricklayer. One day a woman began talking to the bricklayer about how wonderful it was for him to be in the same family as the noted musician. But then, not wanting to insult the bricklayer, she added, "Of course, we don't all have the same talents, and even in the same family some just seem to have more ability than others."

The bricklayer replied, "You're telling me! That violinist brother of mine doesn't know a thing about laying bricks. And if he wasn't able to make some money playing that fiddle of his, he couldn't hire a guy with know-how like mine to build his house. If he had to build a house himself, he'd be ruined."

If you want to build a house, don't look up "violinist" in the yellow pages. And if you need someone to play the violin in an orchestra, don't hire a bricklayer. No two of us are exactly alike, and no one possesses every gift. (HR)

TEMPTATION

MANY OF US SUFFER FROM TEMPTATIONS FROM
WHICH WE HAVE NO BUSINESS TO SUFFER.
—OSWALD CHAMBERS

Ice-Cream Man

Flee also youthful lusts; but pursue righteousness, faith, love, peace with those who call on the Lord out of a pure heart.
—2 *Timothy 2:22*

Little Jeff was trying his best to save money to buy his mother a present. It was a terrible struggle because he gave in so easily to the temptation to buy goodies from the ice-cream man whenever the brightly colored van came through the neighborhood.

One night after his mother had tucked him in bed, she overheard him pray, "Please, God, help me run away when the ice-cream man comes tomorrow." Even at his young age he had learned that one of the best ways to overcome temptation is to avoid what appeals to our weaknesses. (RD)

Victory over Temptation

God is faithful, who will not allow you to be tempted beyond what you are able, but with the temptation will also make the way of escape.   —*1 Corinthians 10:13*

Wanda Johnson, a single mother with five children, was on her way to the pawnshop, where she was hoping to get a loan of sixty dollars for her TV set. Then something bizarre happened. As an armored truck filled with sacks of money drove past her, its rear door flew open, and a bag dropped out. Wanda stopped and picked up the sack. When she counted the cash, she found that it totaled $120,000.

A battle raged in her soul. That money would pay all her bills and provide for the needs of her children. But it wasn't hers to keep.

After a fierce four-hour struggle with her moral convictions, Wanda called the police and turned in the money. Her desire to do the right thing won a victory over the temptation to keep what wasn't hers. (VG)

Orange Peels

Let him who thinks he stands take heed lest he fall.
                                        —*1 Corinthians 10:12*

In 1911, a stuntman named Bobby Leach went over Niagara Falls in a specially designed steel drum—and lived to tell about it. Although he suffered minor injuries, he survived because he recognized the tremendous dangers involved in the feat, and he had done everything he could to protect himself from harm.

Several years later, while walking down a street in New Zealand, Bobby Leach slipped on an orange peel, fell, and badly fractured his leg. He was taken to a hospital, where he died of complications from that fall. He received a greater injury walking down the street than he sustained in going over Niagara Falls because he was not prepared for danger in what he assumed to be a safe situation.

Some of the great temptations that roar around us like the rushing waters of Niagara will leave us unharmed, while a small, seemingly insignificant incident may cause our down-fall. (RD)

The Great Imposter

Put on the whole armor of God, that you may be able to stand against the wiles of the devil. —*Ephesians 6:11*

The arctic polar bear feeds almost entirely on seals. To enjoy such a meal, he sometimes resorts to a cunning bit of trickery. If the hole in the ice through which the seal gets his food is not too far from the edge of open water, the polar bear will take a deep breath, slip underwater, and swim to the seal's fishing hole. He will then imitate a fish by scratching lightly on the underside of the ice. When the seal hears this sound, he dives in for a quick supper, only to find himself suddenly caught in the huge, hungry embrace of his predator.

The Devil entices us in a similar way. He baits us with some seemingly harmless pleasure and disguises the ugliness of sin with something that looks or sounds appealing. Then, when we've succumbed to the temptation, he catches us in his trap. (MD)

TESTIMONY

PREACH THE GOSPEL EVERY DAY; IF NECESSARY, USE WORDS. —ST. FRANCIS OF ASSISI

Nose-Bleed Section

He has delivered us from the power of darkness and conveyed us into the kingdom of the Son of His love. —*Colossians 1:13*

Joe Stowell comments that he has a lot of friends who work in bad neighborhoods. One of these city warriors transplanted his family to the inner city. One day as he was walking down the hallway in his apartment building, he noticed two guys smoking crack cocaine. Not wanting his kids to see what they were doing, he asked the two to stop. The next thing he knew, one of their fists had found its way to his jaw. With a bleeding nose and mouth, he responded, "If Jesus shed His blood for me, I can shed my blood for you."

Shocked by the man's response, the two men fled. A few days later one of them returned, knocked on my friend's door, and said, "I have not forgotten your words. If your God is that real to you, then I want to know Him." (JS)

Stuff Overboard!

What things were gain to me, these I have counted loss for Christ.
—Philippians 3:7

In 1927, John Sung boarded a ship from the U.S. bound for Shanghai. He had been in the States for more than seven years, earning three degrees in that time, including a Ph.D.

As the ship neared its destination, Sung threw all his diplomas, medals, and fraternity keys overboard, keeping only his doctorate diploma to show his father. He had received Jesus Christ and was determined that for the rest of his life he would live only for what counted for eternity.

Many older Christians still living in East and Southeast Asia came to know Christ through the evangelistic ministry of John Sung, who has been called China's Billy Graham. (CPH)

Stolen Car?

Let your light so shine before men, that they may see your good works and glorify your Father in heaven.   *—Matthew 5:16*

Joe Stowell tells the story of the stressed-out woman who was tailgating a man as they drove on a busy boulevard. When the man slowed to a stop at a yellow light, the woman hit the horn, cussing and screaming in frustration and gesturing angrily. As she was still in mid-rant, she heard a tap on her window and looked up into the face of a police officer, who ordered her to exit the car with her hands up. He took her to the police station and placed her in a holding cell.

An hour later, the officer returned and said, "I'm sorry, Ma'am. This has been a big mistake. When I pulled up behind you, I noticed your 'What Would Jesus Do?' license plate holder and your 'Follow Me to Sunday School' bumper sticker. Seeing the way you were acting, I assumed the car was stolen!" (JS)

Earth Walk

The Word became flesh and dwelt among us, and we beheld His glory.
—John 1:14

After the *Apollo XV* mission to the moon, Colonel James Irwin related some of the high points of his experience. He told of the astronauts' weightless bodies floating free in the space capsule, the rising crescent of the earth as seen from the moon, and the triumphal splashdown before a watching world.

Irwin also spoke of the impact the experience had on his spiritual life. He said that from the lunar surface he sensed both the glory of God and the plight of earthbound man. As he came back to earth, he realized he couldn't content himself with being merely a celebrity. He would have to be a servant, telling his fellowman of a better way to live.

Irwin concluded by saying that if we think it a great event to go to the moon, how much greater is the wonder that God came to earth in the person of Jesus Christ! (MD)

What Do You Believe?

The Lord GOD has given Me the tongue of the learned, that I should know how to speak a word in season to him who is weary.
—Isaiah 50:4

Francis Collins earned a Ph.D. in physical chemistry at Yale University and then entered medical school. During his training at a North Carolina hospital, a dying woman often talked to him about her faith in Christ. He rejected the existence of God, but he couldn't ignore the woman's serenity.

One day she asked, "What do you believe?"

Caught off guard, Collins' face turned red as he stammered, "I'm not really sure."

A few days later the woman died.

Curious and uneasy, the young doctor realized that he had rejected God without adequately examining the evidence. He began to read the Bible and the writings of C. S. Lewis. A year later he fell to his knees and gave his life to Jesus Christ. The catalyst? A sincere question from an elderly woman whose physical heart was failing but whose concern for others was strong. (DM)

Inside Out

[Jesus] said, "What comes out of a man, that defiles a man."
—*Mark 7:20*

While giving a sermon, missionary Hudson Taylor filled a glass with water and placed it on a table in front of him. As he was speaking, he pounded his fist hard enough to make the water splash onto the table. He then explained, "You will come up against much trouble. But when you do, remember, only what's in you will spill out." (RD)

Say So

Let us continually offer the sacrifice of praise to God, that is, the fruit of our lips, giving thanks to His name.   —*Hebrews 13:15*

Mel Trotter was a drunken barber whose salvation not only turned his own life around but also changed thousands of others. He was saved in 1897 in Chicago at the Pacific Garden Mission, and not long afterward he was named director of the City Rescue Mission in Grand Rapids, Michigan.

Thirty-five years later, at a meeting at the mission, Mel Trotter was conducting "Say-So" time. He asked people in the crowd to testify how Jesus had saved them. A fourteen-year-old boy stood up and said simply, "I'm glad Jesus saved me. Amen."

Trotter remarked, "That's the finest testimony I ever heard."

Encouraged by those words from such an important leader, that teenager, Mel Johnson, went on to become a Christian leader in his own right as a pioneer in Christian radio. His name lives on today at Northwestern College in St. Paul, Minnesota, at the Mel Johnson Media Center.

Young Mel was encouraged to say so, and he did. Six little words, followed by an encouraging comment. A testimony and an affirmation led to a life of service for God. (DB)

A Helping Hand

To him who is afflicted, kindness should be shown by his friend.
—Job 6:14

A college student named Kelly shattered her arm in the first volleyball game of the season. This meant she couldn't work at her part-time job. Then her car stopped running. To top it all off, the young man she had been dating stopped calling. Kelly felt so low that she began spending hours alone in her room crying.

Laura, a Christian friend on the volleyball team, became concerned about Kelly and decided to help her. So she planned a party. She and some friends collected money, and a couple of guys got Kelly's car running again. They found a temporary job she could do using just one hand. And they gave her tickets to see her basketball hero when his team came to town.

Before long, Kelly was herself again. When she asked why they did all this for her, Laura was able to tell her about the love of Jesus. (DE)

THANKFULNESS

FEELING GRATITUDE AND NOT EXPRESSING IT IS LIKE
WRAPPING A PRESENT AND NOT GIVING IT.
—WILLIAM ARTHUR WARD

Whose Prisoner?

This grace was given, that I should preach among the Gentiles the unsearchable riches of Christ. —Ephesians 3:8

A story is told of Scottish minister Alexander Whyte, who was able to look at the bleakest situation and yet find something to be thankful for. On a dark Sunday morning when the weather was freezing, wet, and stormy, one of his deacons whispered, "I am sure the preacher won't be able to thank God for anything on a day like this. It's absolutely horrible outside!"

Pastor Whyte began the service by praying, "We thank Thee, O God, that the weather is not always like this." (AL)

Did You Thank God Today?

Enter into His gates with thanksgiving, and into His courts with praise. Be thankful to Him, and bless His name. —Psalm 100:4

On his way to work one day, Dennis De Haan saw a bumper sticker that read: "Did you thank a green plant today?"

Plants are essential to the balance of nature. They release oxygen into the air. They're also a source of food, fuel, medicine, and building materials.

Was the bumper sticker suggesting that because we are so dependent on plants we should actually thank them? If that's what the driver believes, he certainly has a lot to learn about who should receive our gratitude.

Nature bears marvelous testimony to the wisdom of the Creator. The interdependence of one life form on another makes us realize that we're part of a complex system characterized by beauty and balance. But to direct our praise to nature reminds us of Paul's indictment of those who "worshiped and served the creature rather than the Creator" (Romans 1:25). (DD)

God Is Alive!

O Lord my God, I will give thanks to You forever. —Psalm 30:12

The great sixteenth-century theologian Martin Luther once experienced a long period of worry and despondency. One day he was surprised to find his wife dressed in black mourning clothes.

"Who has died?" asked Luther.

"God," said his wife.

"God!" said Luther, horrified. "How can you say such a thing?"

She replied, "I'm only saying what you are living."

Luther realized that he indeed was living as if God were no longer alive and watching over them in love. He changed his outlook from gloom to gratitude. (JY)

A Lost Art

Let the peace of God rule in your hearts... and be thankful.
—Colossians 3:15

Warren Wiersbe told about a ministerial student in Evanston, Illinois, who was part of a life-saving squad. In 1860, a ship went aground on the shore of Lake Michigan near Evanston, and Edward Spencer waded again and again into the frigid waters to rescue seventeen passengers. In the process, his health was permanently damaged. Some years later at his funeral, it was noted that not one of the people he rescued ever thanked him. (DE)

TRUSTING GOD

Everlasting Arms

The eternal God is your refuge, and underneath are the everlasting arms.   —*Deuteronomy 33:27*

After a pre-concert rehearsal in New York City's Carnegie Hall, Randall Atcheson sat on stage alone. He had successfully navigated the intricate piano compositions of Beethoven, Chopin, and Liszt for the evening program, and with only minutes remaining before the doors opened, he wanted to play one more piece for himself. What came from his heart and his hands was an old hymn by Elisha Hoffman:

> What have I to dread,
> What have I to fear,
> Leaning on the everlasting arms?
> I have blessed peace
> With my Lord so near,
> Leaning on the everlasting arms. (DM)

Deep Water

Let not the floodwater overflow me, nor let the deep swallow me up.   —*Psalm 69:15*

The builders of sport utility vehicles (SUVs) like to show us their products in mind-boggling situations. High on a mountain crag, where no truck could seemingly go. Or in a swamp so impassable you'd need a hovercraft to negotiate it. We're supposed to think that SUVs are invincible.

That's why there seems to be some unintended humor in the disclaimer in a recent ad for a four-wheel-drive SUV. A photo showed the vehicle up to its headlights in water as it forged across a foreboding river. The ad said: "Traversing deep water can cause damage, which voids the vehicle warranty." (DB)

It's in God's Hands

"Vengeance is Mine, I will repay," says the Lord. —Romans 12:19

The world was horrified when Chechen rebels massacred hundreds of people held hostage in a school in Beslan, Russia. Many of the victims were children, including six belonging to the two Totiev brothers, who are active in Christian ministry.

One of the brothers reacted in a way that most of us would have a hard time choosing. He said, "Yes, we have an irreplaceable loss, but we cannot take revenge." He believes what the Lord says, "Vengeance is Mine, I will repay." (VG)

WARNING

ONE THORN OF EXPERIENCE IS WORTH A WHOLE WILDERNESS OF WARNING. —JAMES RUSSELL LOWELL

What Volcano?

Be ready, for the Son of Man is coming at an hour you do not expect.
—Matthew 24:44

Rising 2,900 meters (9,600 feet) above the rain forest in Indonesia's southern Java, Mount Merapi (the Fire Mountain) is one of the world's most dangerous volcanoes.

As the Fire Mountain showed signs of renewed activity, authorities tried to evacuate local residents. Then, on May 13, 2006, Merapi spewed a gray plume of sulfurous smoke that resembled a flock of sheep leaving the crater. Amazingly, villagers ignored the signs and returned to tending their livestock, apparently forgetting that in 1994 Merapi had killed sixty people.

It's our human tendency to ignore signs. (CPH)

Heed the Warning

These things... were written for our admonition.
—1 Corinthians 10:11

In the months following the devastating Asian tsunami of December 2004, an amazing story of survival emerged from Simeulue Island, the closest inhabited land to the epicenter of the earthquake.

A news report said that only seven of the remote Indonesian island's 75,000 inhabitants died when thirty-foot waves struck just half an hour after the quake. For decades, the people had heard stories told by their grandparents of giant waves that killed thousands on this same island in 1907. So when the ground shook and the sea retreated from the shore, the people recalled their grandparents' warnings and fled to high ground. (DM)

It's a Long Story

He who is often rebuked, and hardens his neck, will suddenly be destroyed. *—Proverbs 29:1*

In August 1989, a major fire broke out under an elevated section of New Jersey's Interstate 78. The intense heat buckled parts of the highway and forced the closing of the East Coast artery. The governor said it was the worst transportation crisis in years.

An investigation brought to light a longstanding problem. It revealed that the fire broke out in a dumpsite in which construction debris had been collecting for many years. The owners of the site had been convicted of a multimillion-dollar conspiracy to allow the illegal dumping of construction debris. But appeals in federal and state courts frustrated New Jersey's efforts to clean up the area. Not until the day after the fire did a state appeals court finally order the operator of the dump to stop accepting trash and begin clearing the site.

Like the fire at that dumpsite, most of our problems don't just happen. They are the result of a long series of bad decisions. (MD)

Old Skinflint

Let each one give as he purposes in his heart, not grudgingly or of necessity; for God loves a cheerful giver. —2 Corinthians 9:7

Some people will do anything to save a buck, like the miserly uncle that Dave Egner read about. He invited his nephews to hunt for arrowheads in the field behind his house. Before the search could begin, however, he told the excited youngsters they had to move all the rocks out of the field and clear away the underbrush. By the time they were finished, it was too late to search for arrowheads. Later, they learned that none had ever been found on his property. When they complained to their dad, he said, "My old skinflint brother bamboozled you out of a day's work."

There's nothing wrong with being frugal. It's a matter of good stewardship. But there is something wrong with being so thrifty that you take advantage of others or won't pay a boy what he's worth. We're to be fair, giving, and generous people. (DE)

A Storm Is Coming

It is appointed for men to die once, but after this the judgment.
—Hebrews 9:27

Dr. M. R. De Haan and a fishing buddy were in a small boat on the far side of the lake, and the fish were biting. When they heard a rumble of thunder in the distance, they looked up and saw a mass of dark clouds in the west.

The Doctor ignored the suggestion of his fishing partner that it might be wise to start back to the cottage—he wanted to keep fishing. Then it happened! The storm was suddenly upon them. They tried to start the motor, but it wouldn't go! His friend tried to row, but the rain came in sheets and the waves tossed their little aluminum boat.

The two of them survived, but Dr. De Haan learned a lesson. Don't delay when a storm is brewing. (MRD)

WISDOM

SOME FOLKS ARE WISE AND SOME ARE OTHERWISE.
—TOBIAS SMOLLETT

Searching for a Rare Jewel

Happy is the man who finds wisdom... for her proceeds are better than the profits of silver, and her gain than fine gold.
—*Proverbs 3:13–14*

When Betty Goldstein of Staten Island, New York, entered the hospital, her husband Ron wrapped her 3.5-carat diamond ring in a napkin for safekeeping. But in a forgetful moment, Goldstein threw the napkin in the trash. When he realized his mistake, he dashed outside, only to see the garbage truck rumbling down the street. So he called the local sanitation department and got permission to follow the truck to a transfer station. Workers began sorting through hundreds of garbage bags and recovered the ring an hour later.

The writer of Proverbs urges us to search diligently for something far more precious—wisdom. (MW)

Trivial Pursuits

His divine power has given to us all things that pertain to life and godliness. —2 Peter 1:3

A number of years ago David Roper was in the library of a prestigious university. As he walked among the bookshelves, he happened to pass by a row of small cubicles set aside for study and spied a student reading a Bugs Bunny comic book. Roper says he almost laughed out loud. Here was a young man surrounded by the wisdom of the ages, yet immersed in childish trivia. (DR)

Let's Talk About It

Let not mercy and truth forsake you; bind them around your neck, write them on the tablet of your heart. —Proverbs 3:3

The police in San Diego, California, received complaints from a woman who said she was getting annoying phone calls. In the middle of the night a person would phone her, bark like a dog, and then hang up.

Police eventually discovered that the source of the calls was a neighbor. He said that whenever he was awakened by the barking of her dog, he wanted to make sure she was awake too.

The neighbor's approach might have been imaginative, but it certainly wasn't merciful or wise. At the right time and for the sake of all parties involved, an honest discussion is usually part of the solution. (MD)

The Wisdom of the Word

Where is the wise? Where is the scribe? ... Has not God made foolish the wisdom of this world? —1 Corinthians 1:20

Vernon Grounds says he was glad to read an article by *New York Times* columnist David Brooks extolling biblical wisdom. Brooks praised Martin Luther King Jr. for insight into human nature derived from Scripture. He felt that King "had a more accurate view of political realities than his more secular liberal

155

allies because he could draw on biblical wisdom about human nature. Religion didn't just make civil rights leaders stronger—it made them smarter."

And Brooks said further: "Biblical wisdom is deeper and more accurate than the wisdom offered by the secular social sciences." (VG)

Multitude of Counselors

In the multitude of counselors there is safety. —Proverbs 11:14

In October 1962, the world held its breath as the U.S. and the Soviet Union stood at the brink of nuclear war. Premier Nikita Khrushchev had delivered nuclear missiles to Cuba, and President John F. Kennedy demanded their immediate removal. Tensions between the two nations were at an all-time high.

President Kennedy phoned three former U.S. presidents to get their advice. Herbert Hoover had faced the economic problems of the Great Depression; Harry Truman had ended World War II; and Dwight Eisenhower had served as the Supreme Allied Commander in Europe during World War II. Each had valuable insights to share. After Kennedy conferred with all of his White House advisors, a balanced course of action defused the crisis. War was averted.

The Bible encourages us to seek the advice of wise counselors. (DF)

What's Worth Keeping

For one morsel of food [Esau] sold his birthright. —Hebrews 12:16

A story is told of a man who loved old books. He met an acquaintance who had just thrown away a Bible that had been stored in the attic of his ancestral home for generations. "I couldn't read it," the friend explained. "Somebody named Guten-something had printed it."

"Not Gutenberg!" the book lover exclaimed in horror. "That Bible was one of the first books ever printed. A copy just sold for over two million dollars!"

His friend was unimpressed. "Mine wouldn't have brought a dollar. Some fellow named Martin Luther had scribbled all over it in German."

This fictitious story shows how an unwise person can treat as worthless that which is valuable. (HR)

OUR DAILY BREAD
WRITERS

Henry Bosch (HB)

Dave Branon (DB)

Anne Cetas (AC)

Bill Crowder (BC)

Dennis De Haan (DD)

Mart De Haan (MD)

Dr. M. R. De Haan (MRD)

Richard De Haan (RD)

Dave Egner (DE)

Dennis Fisher (DF)

Vernon Grounds (VG)

Tim Gustafson (TG)

C. P. Hia (CPH)

Cindy Hess Kasper (CHK)

Albert Lee (AL)

Julie Ackerman Link (JAL)

David McCasland (DM)

Haddon Robinson (HR)

David Roper (DR)

Joe Stowell (JS)

Paul Van Gorder (PVG)

Herb Vander Lugt (HVL)

Marvin Williams (MW)

Joanie Yoder (JY)

For biographical information about each of the *ODB* writers, check online at www.rbc.org

NOTE TO THE READER

The publisher invites you to share your response to the message of this book by writing Discovery House Publishers, P.O. Box 3566, Grand Rapids, MI 49501, U.S. For information about other Discovery House books, music, videos, or DVDs, contact us at the same address or call 1-800-653-8333. Find us on the Internet at http://www.dhp.org/ or send e-mail to books@dhp.org.